MIGRANT
MARSEILLE

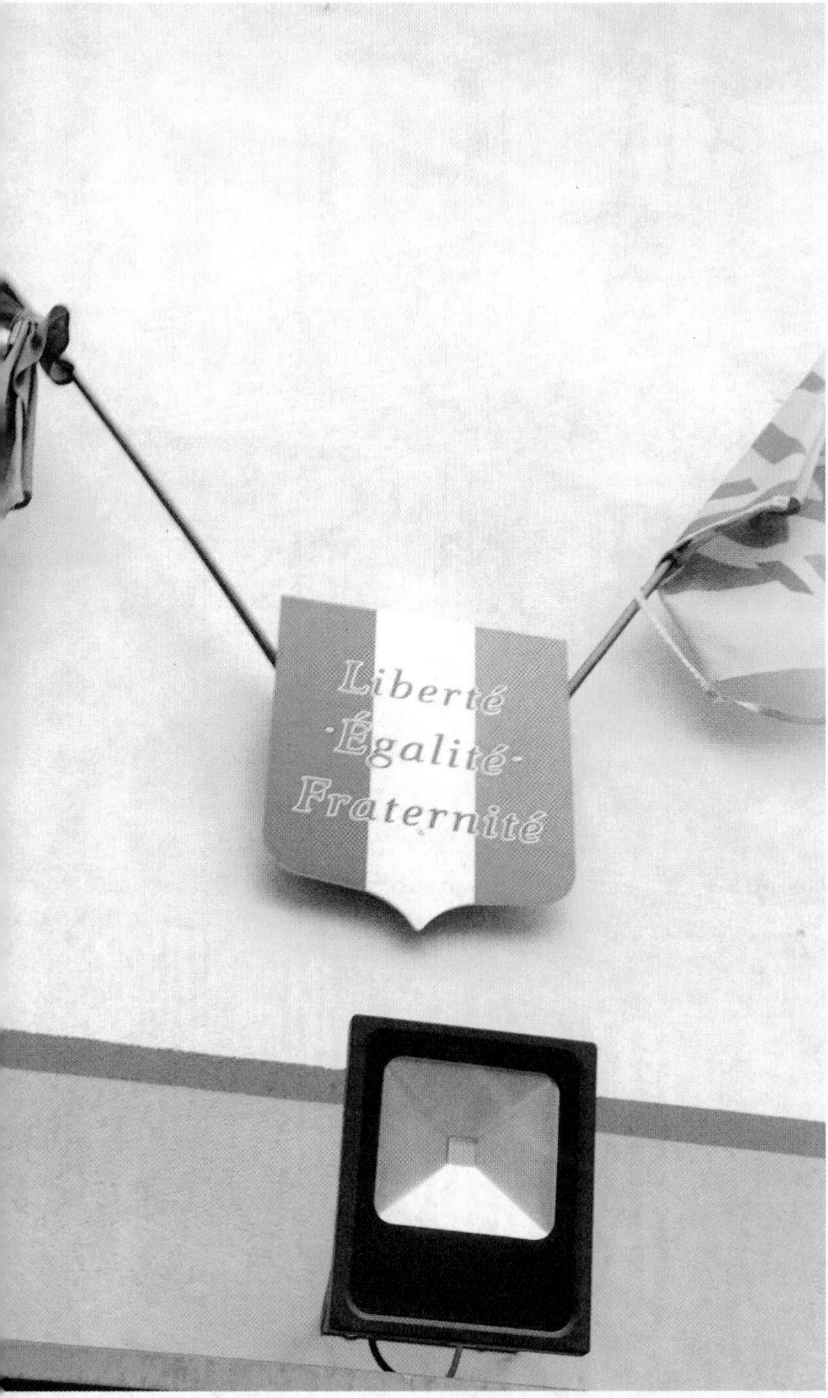
Liberté
·Égalité·
Fraternité

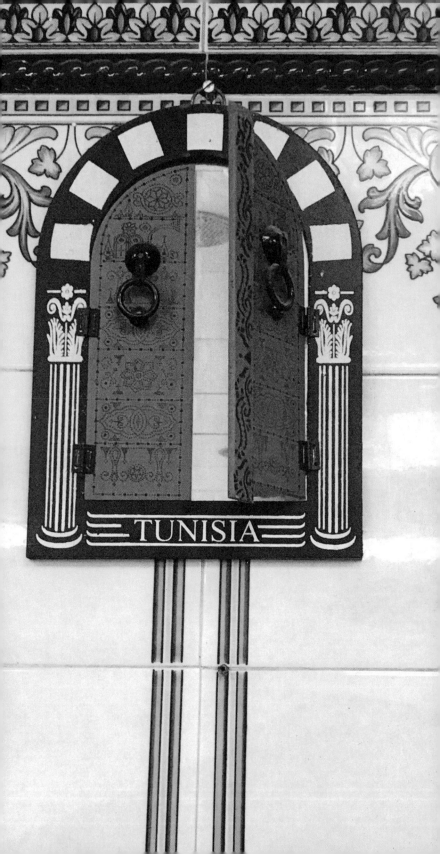

ETH ZURICH
MAS URBAN DESIGN

MIGRANT MARSEILLE

ARCHITECTURES OF SOCIAL SEGREGATION AND URBAN INCLUSIVITY

EDITED BY
MARC ANGÉLIL
CHARLOTTE MALTERRE-BARTHES
AND SOMETHING FANTASTIC

RUBY PRESS

MARSEILLE: IS THERE A CITY BEYOND THE CLICHÉS?

Introduction

Charlotte Malterre-Barthes

Migration as Urban Identity

Tourism guides are not kind to Marseille. Indeed, The Rough Guide to Provence & the Côte d'Azur's summary is symptomatic of the city's poor reputation: "Marseille has all the social, economic and political tensions of France writ large. To some extent it is a divided city, with the ethnic French living on one side of La Canebiére, and the large, vibrant North African community on the other side: needless to say, racism is rife, as are poverty, bad housing and rising unemployment, particularly among the youth."[1] A 2,600-year-old port located on the Mediterranean shores of France, Marseille was established by Greek sailors as a harbor city with few connections to its hinterland, and developed as a trading hub favoring overseas exchanges over inland trade. Historically, Marseille's politics has reflected an outsider's position, challenging ruling powers, such as supporting Pompey over Rome, countering Louis XIV or Napoleon, and setting against the Thiers government during the Commune. Despite being cliché-ridden, images of Marseille form what urbanist Marcel Roncayolo calls an imaginary (*imaginaire*), that is, an agglomeration of individual and collective images throughout history, language, and landscapes as common signs or perceptions, contributing to memory as individual psychology.[2] This imaginary is the substance of the city—from which

William Firebrace crafted the book *Marseille Mix*, made of urban stories.[3] A city, through its architecture, urbanism, infrastructure, institutions, and monuments, as well as its everyday images and relational networks, creates a multi-scalar mental territory that changes through time.

Marseille, harbor city, city harbor, projects at the end of the eighteenth century a somewhat exaggerated image of an isolated city close to the African continent, living off maritime exchanges. With the economic crisis of the nineteenth century, the city's imaginary becomes provincial, limiting spaces and functions. The greatness of Marseille then concentrates on industrial economy and colonial activities. At the turn of the nineteenth century, the city is industrial as well as popular, and embodies visions of a hard-working labor force, tight human relations, close sociability, and everyday cosmopolitanism.[4] It functions as an articulation between local, national, and global scales, with colonialism as a link. It is not before the late 1970s and the 1980s that a new imaginary emerges, with crime and mafia organizations painting Marseille as a Mediterranean island, sister in crime to Corsica and Sicily (i.e., Judge Michel's murder and the "French connection"), turned again toward the sea.[5]

Overlapping with this territory's imaginary, is the more trivial, affective, even sentimental picture of Marseille—which one could also call identity—founded in sports, music, and political views, and built against Paris as the ruling symbol of French authority. Residents tend to say they are "Marseillais before anything else." In the late 1990s, a rich hip-hop and reggae milieu developed in the northern and central districts, with songs whose lyrics were critical of both local and national governance politics, and which established a dual identity immigrant and as inhabitant of Marseille.[6 7 8] The local football team, Olympique de Marseille, is revered. Internationally renowned Zinedine Zidane, born in the so-called Quartiers Nord (a term used to discriminate against the northern districts of the city) to an Algerian family who lived in the Cité la Castellane, for a decade smiled from a giant poster on the Corniche Kennedy, the coastal road south of the city. But football, as a so-called miracle that would unite all social classes for matches at the Stade Vélodrome, reproduces the social divisions of the city in the tribune placements within the stadium. However, it too contributes to the collective imaginary as a space of commoning and centrality. This imaginary as an empirical factor is rooted in time and fluctuates in a large chronological frame that is given and belongs to the inhabitants, whether newcomers or longtime locals. Perhaps the identification phenomenon that is the feeling of belonging contributes to maintaining the precarious imbalance between a beloved city and a hated state (as a long-established enemy) and possibly mitigating socio-political tensions.[9]

"They were from Marseille before being Arabs. [...] That's what it was, the story of Marseille. Its eternity. Its utopia. The only utopia of the world. A place where anybody of any color could come off a boat or a train, suitcase in hand and pockets empty, and merge into the flow of other humans. A city where, the second that one stepped onto the ground, one could say: 'That's it. I'm home.' Marseille belongs to those who live there."[10] This excerpt from Jean-Claude Izzo's crime stories paints a somewhat idyllic portrait of the city that can be easily dismissed as naive. Yet it illustrates how immigration is key to Marseille's image and identity, not only as a strong empirical component of the city's imaginary, but as a real economic motor that has shaped the city's social and urban structure for centuries.

Migrant Marseille

This is a publication interested in two types of relationships: first, how migration relates to and plays out in space, architecture, and territory, between social and spatial arrangements; and second, how design can work with and react to these sites and conditions. It argues that migration is the ideal entry point into an engaged form of spatial practice and design agency. Migration is neither a new phenomenon nor a specifically modern condition. In the quest for a better, safer life, people have always moved. But in the wake of Europe's refugee crisis and the climate emergency, it has become a pressing topic. Circulations of people, goods, and capital, as much as their resettlement, have a visible, transformative impact upon space at various scales. Aiming to uncover architectures of social segregation and urban inclusivity, this work attempts to address the relational dynamics between migration and the built environment, and how space—from architecture to territory—is shaped by, and in turn shapes, political, economic, and social practices. However, *Migrant Marseille* does not pretend to grasp such a broad matter in its entirety. Instead, it chooses to narrate an urban reality, where migration is present at every turn, in a myriad of ways.

The section "A Brief History of Housing and Migration, 1800–1975," introduces a city where newcomers have played an essential

role in shaping the socioeconomic face of the territory, but where state responses have been ambiguous. An examination of several housing estates reveals a rich modernist architectural heritage in various environments, from Le Corbusier's Unité d'Habitation to Alvar Aalto's forest town–inspired Le Roy d'Espagne. It is enriched by "Marseille, the Great Move," a record of the architectural production in the political context of the time, by architect Thierry Durousseau.

"Neighborhoods" are then investigated to better understand the urban and architectural fabric. These function as urban probes to tell the ongoing story of migrant Marseille and address a specific problematic: Belsunce, the arrival neighborhood; Noailles, the diverse but afflicted district; Félix Pyat and La Castellane, the Comorian- and Algerian-rich housing estates under police control and demolition programs; La Rouvière, the *pieds-noirs*' segregated haven; Parc Kallisté, the dilapidated co-ownership home to illegal newcomers; and concluding with the zone within the Euroméditerranée urban redevelopment program under threat of gentrification. Quotations and texts from the media, militants, and residents punctuate the book, making space for local voices and contentious dialogues. Homegrown activist and urbanist Nicolas Memain delivers a vivid contextual account of the city today in "Marseille at War," and Marc Angélil and Cary Siress take a philosophical yet critical stance toward the banlieues in "La Marseillaise for All?"

In "Projects for Marseille," student works deploy strategies and tactics to address the pressing questions posed by each of the sites, with a focus on inclusivity. The final section of "Principles, Tools, and Ideas for an Inclusive Urbanism" presents distilled, illustrated thoughts that support planning and design in a more inclusive way. The essay "The Possibilities of an Inclusive Urbanism" by me and Something Fantastic concludes the publication.

Undertaken by the students of the Master of Advanced Studies in Urban Design at the chair of Marc Angélil (Department of Architecture, ETH Zurich), under my direction with Something Fantastic, *Migrant Marseille* encourages architects and planners to take into account all social, spatial, and ecological factors in their work. Presenting alternatives to conventional planning methods and concerns, it aims to redefine urban design as a discipline that holds the key to new visions of a more just, planet-conscious, and heterogeneous built environment.

1   *The Rough Guide to Provence & the Côte d'Azur* (London: Penguin Books, 2007), 61.
2   Marcel Roncayolo, *Lectures de villes: Formes et temps* (Marseille: Editions Parenthèses, 2002), 358.
3   William Firebrace, *Marseille Mix* (London: AA Publications, 2010).
4   Albert Londres, *Marseille, porte du sud* (Paris: Arléa, 1999), 120.
5   Alfred W. McCoy, *Marseille sur héroïne* (Paris: L'Esprit Frappeur, 1999), 158.
6   "Immigrant" is a disputed term, as it assembles the just-arrived population as well as the first, second, third, or fourth generations of immigrants, French citizens born in France. "Of immigrant origin" is also used in the media, but is questionable as well, as it often only concerns North Africans. The term immigrant is used in this text to mean foreign nationals settled in France.
7   The northern districts (Quartiers Nord), north of the Canebière axis, is where most of the *habitations à loyer modéré* (rent-controlled housing, HLM) and *grands ensembles* are situated.
8   See, for instance, the songs "Planète Mars" by IAM, "Belsunce Breakdown" by Bouga, and "Chourmo!" by Massilia Sound System.
9   It is believed by many scholars that in France, violence is due to a loss of confidence in institutions and the role they traditionally play in the integration process of new populations. Therefore, violence tends to be aimed at amenities and public institutions, the state and its representatives. See, for instance, Laurent Bonelli, "Les raisons d'une colère," *Manière de voir*, October–November 2006, 6.
10 Jean-Claude Izzo, *Total Khéops*, Série Noire (Paris: Éditions Gallimard, 1995).

C. Castaner, Minister of Interior Affairs:

"Our immigration policy is based on two pillars: to generously welcome those who are threatened and make a legal and legitimate asylum request, and to effectively remove those who are in an irregular situation. It is a balance that we must preserve. It is the honor of the Republic to welcome the most vulnerable people, the most in danger: to welcome refugees. We must give them the chance of real integration, through work, housing, learning the language and values of the Republic. This is the road map that I set myself and that I am proud to lead. Integration is a subject of cohesion and responsibility, which requires the commitment of all, and postures do not have their place." [1]

S. Frédéric, member of the Ancrages association:

"Through the history of Marseille, phases of acceptance and rejection of the migration phenomenon have alternated. [...] We need to look more in detail at the definitions of the different terms: migrant, immigrant, refugee. When we talk about 'a migrant' we refer to a person that is in motion; the focus is on displacement. In France and in Marseille, this notion implies a temporary and transient condition. Therefore the migrant community is disadvantaged, for example it does not receive adequate housing. [...] Looking at our industrial heritage, we can see that migrants were and still are an important source of labor, and looking at our residential heritage, we can see that migrants left important traces on the city landscape. We also investigate the struggles and collective mobilizations of migrant laborers in the city." [2]

1   C. Castaner, "Le dispositif," Minister of
    Interior Affairs, June 20, 2019.

2   S. Frédéric, interview by MAS Urban
    Design, Marseille, March 19, 2019.

HOTEL SQUARE
LOUISE MICHEL

Louise MICHEL
1830-1905

A
BRIEF
HISTORY
OF
HOUSING
AND
MIGRATION
1800–1975

MIGRATION, PUBLIC POLICIES, HOUSING

The Construction of Marseille's Uneven Geography 1800s–2000s

In the second-largest French city—a trading port founded in 600 BC by Greeks from Phocaea—harbor activities and constant migratory flows have shaped the physical, social, and economic geography, particularly the successive immigration waves of the past century.[1] France has long been a country of immigration, and authorities long considered this permanent condition as temporary. Housing programs reflected this, paving the way for an ethnic segregation which was to greatly affect the socio-spatial geography of French cities, Marseille in particular. Chronicling migration waves and the public response to housing sheds light on the socio-spatial landscape of the city today, and why Marseille presents such a divide between the wealthy southern districts and the impoverished northern neighborhoods—stigmatized under the name Quartiers Nord, of which the city's central artery, La Canebière, forms a blurred but unequivocal border.

Nineteenth Century to World War I: Italians and Kabyles

Starting in the 1830s with the colonization of Algeria and the construction of the Paris–Lyon–Marseille railway, Marseille became the leading port for colonial businesses in France. As the harbor expanded north of the city for industrial activities (i.e., sugar, soap, tile factories), this economic boom attracted migrant labor, mainly from Italy. These migrants, along with modest French workers, settled in the northern peripheral areas of the city. Here, workers were either offered simple provisional housing by their companies or they lived in overcrowded, self-built bidonvilles. On the opposite side of the city, the bourgeoisie established itself in the southern districts, as wealthy traders bought plots of land to build luxurious homes away from the factories' dirt and labor forces.[2] Meanwhile, workers unionized and formed inter-ethnic social groups, supporting strikes and protests for better wages

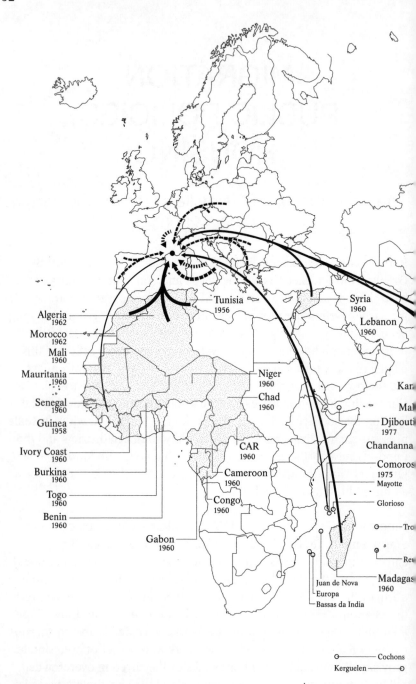

Tunisia
1956

Syria
1960

Lebanon
1960

Algeria
1962

Morocco
1962

Mali
1960

Mauritania
1960

Senegal
1960

Guinea
1958

Ivory Coast
1960

Burkina
1960

Togo
1960

Benin
1960

Gabon
1960

Niger
1960

Chad
1960

CAR
1960

Cameroon
1960

Congo
1960

Kar

Mal

Djibouti
1977

Chandanna

Comoros
1975

Mayotte

Glorioso

Tro

Rev

Madagas
1960

Juan de Nova

Europa

Bassas da India

Cochons

Kerguelen

Marseille Migration History

⚬⚬⚬⚬⚬⚬ "The Italian invasion" (1850–1914)

▬▬▬▬ Diversification of migration flows (1928–1941)

▬▬▬ Decolonization and African immigration (1950–now)

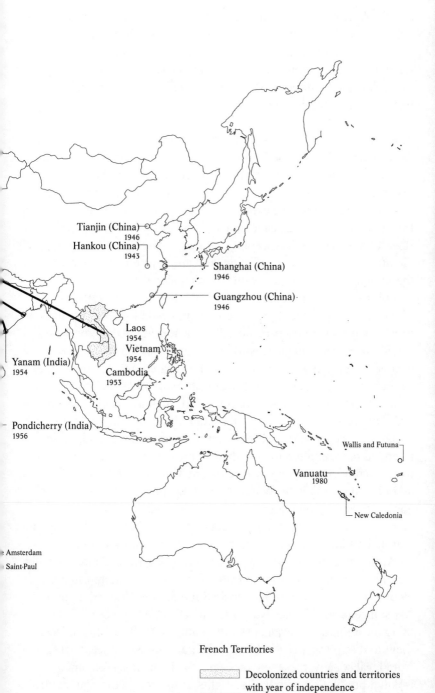

Tianjin (China)
1946
Hankou (China)
1943
Shanghai (China)
1946
Guangzhou (China)
1946
Laos
1954
Vietnam
1954
Yanam (India)
1954
Cambodia
1953
Pondicherry (India)
1956
Wallis and Futuna
Vanuatu
1980
New Caledonia
Amsterdam
Saint-Paul

French Territories

Decolonized countries and territories
with year of independence
Departments and overseas territories

and working conditions. Around 1910, these recurrent confrontations led Marseille's industries to turn to France's North African colonies to recruit workers, mainly from the Algerian region of Kabylia. They were hired as strikebreakers, fueling conflicts among the working class to weaken its contractual power, and resulting in their marginalization from their fellow laborers.

The Interwar Period: Ethnic Diversification
At the outbreak of World War I, as many Italians were leaving and the French labor force integrating into the military, public authorities urgently engaged in the recruitment of workers from the colonies. As the war ended, Marseille experienced a second wave of migration, this time fueled by political conflicts; Russians fleeing the October Revolution, Armenians escaping genocide, Spaniards leaving Franco's dictatorship, all in search of safety and employment. To cope with the humanitarian emergency, the municipality set up transit camps and barracks that could house hundreds. During the 1930s, the French government and private companies established a recruitment program and institutions responsible for housing and medical care for foreign workers. The guest workers' regime was based on differential exclusion: foreign workers were accommodated only temporarily as economic subjects, and excluded socially, culturally, and politically.[3] Isolated forms of housing were preferred, such as workers' villages or *cités-jardins,* where workers could retain their cultural, religious, and social practices during their temporary stay in France—an isolation intended to facilitate return to their home countries. Further workers from neighboring nations also settled in Marseille and gradually assimilated into French society. Arrival neighborhoods, such as Le Panier, Belsunce, and later Noailles were crucial to that process. Here, immigrants could rely on social networks based on kinship and national affiliation to find accommodation and employment.[4]

At the time, workers from the colonies were treated more harshly, having to comply with stricter rules. Their stay was administered by organizations such as Service de Surveillance, Protection, et Assistance des Indigènes Nord-Africain (SAINA) and Service de l'Organisation des Travailleurs Coloniaux (SOTC), which subjected them to disciplinary control under the guise of assistance. Segregated from local society, these workers—mostly single men—remained an isolated population with limited rights, subjected to the tight control of authorities.

Post–World War II: North African Migration

After World War II, Marseille, like the rest of France, engaged in physical reconstruction and the revival of economic activities, a period later known as the Glorious Thirty (1945–1975). To gather the necessary workforce for this national effort, another guest-worker scheme was established, one that would last until the 1973 oil crisis. At first, workers overwhelmingly arrived from Algeria and other colonized North African countries, like Morocco. No housing facilities were constructed for these laborers and their families, and informal Algerian bidonvilles sprouted up, clustering around the industries that employed them, largely on the northern side of the city close to transport infrastructure. After the beginning of Algeria's war of independence in 1956, these migrant workers were considered a threat. In order to contain political unrest, the government established the Société Nationale de Construction de Logements pour les Travailleurs Algériens (SONACOTRAL), an institution intended to build and manage shelters exclusively for Algerian workers.[5]

When Algeria gained its independence, thousands of *pieds-noirs*—French natives, *colons*, living in Algeria—arrived in Marseille. They settled first in hotels, and then found housing in the private market in some of the large-scale housing projects (*grands ensembles*), like La Rouvière. However, most of the newly built residential complexes that both state and private developers constructed were primarily intended to house the growing population of the French metropolis and solve the postwar housing crisis, rather than accommodate newcomers.[6] In parallel, native Algerians continued to arrive, and racial tensions arose across the city. As colonial biases infiltrated the political apparatus, these populations were portrayed as uncivilized and ill-prepared for the cohabitation of social housing. Authorities thus decided *émigrés* had to prove their sociability before being eligible for a subsidized apartment, creating basic residential estates for them, known as *cités de transit*.[7] After two years in a *cité*, families were to be rehoused in flats in an *habitation à loyer modéré* (rent-controlled housing, HLM); however, this was seldom realized. Many stayed for over a decade in such emergency camps, located at the periphery of the city. During these years, ethnic segregation was exacerbated by the poor political and economic choices of the city's administration.[8]

On the one hand, favoritism and corruption became prevalent practices; for decades, Marseille's mayors administered the city by exchanging municipal employment for votes, resulting in an increase of

Emergency and provisional cités and bidonvilles

public jobs still palpable today.[9] On the other hand, after the national independences of the 1960s, the city's port economy suffered a steady decline. Marine traffic–related industrial activities were relocated to a neighboring city, Fos-sur-Mer.[10] The combination of an overinflated public sector and the disappearance of industrial activities hindered the economic development of the city and the well-being of its local and foreign population. During this time, large amounts of municipal funds were allocated to develop the southern districts and improve the vehicular-traffic network. Middle-class residents in the inner city and the north were encouraged to move to newly built single-family properties in the south and east. The northern neighborhoods, already home to industries, the working class, and immigrants, saw the construction of 90 percent of the city's social housing projects. This is where migrants from Morocco, sub-Saharan Africa, and the Caribbean were to move into long-coveted HLM apartment blocks, such as La Castellane and Parc Kallisté. Some *cités* over time became home to a homogeneous community, like Félix Pyat, whose residents are overwhelmingly from the Comoros—a French colony until 1975. As French lower-class citizens gained financial stability and accessed homeownership, they vacated the *grands ensembles*, and migrants moved in. After the oil crisis of 1973, the French economy entered a recession period, forcing migrant workers to return. Following the phasing out of the guest workers' regime, immigration flows dried up, only to be fueled again by family reunification policies, a legal right since 1976. The combination of these forms of continued immigration into the large public housing projects in the northern districts was to have a tremendous and long-lasting effect on the social and physical landscape of Marseille.

Current Situation

During the 1980s, 1990s, and 2000s, France was shaken by urban unrest in these neglected neighborhoods. The state decided to implement a series of measures called Politique de la Ville. This new bureaucratic apparatus relied on two administrative instruments. The first was the Contract de Ville (1989), a three-year agreement between central government and municipalities, instituted with the purpose of transferring funds to troubled neighborhoods (*quartiers en difficulté*). The second tool was the Pacte de Reliance Sociale (1996),[11] which defined three geographical levels of intervention at a municipal scale: *zone urbaine sensible* (ZUS), *zone de redynamisation urbaine* (ZRU), and *zone franche urbaine* (ZFU).[12] These measures were set

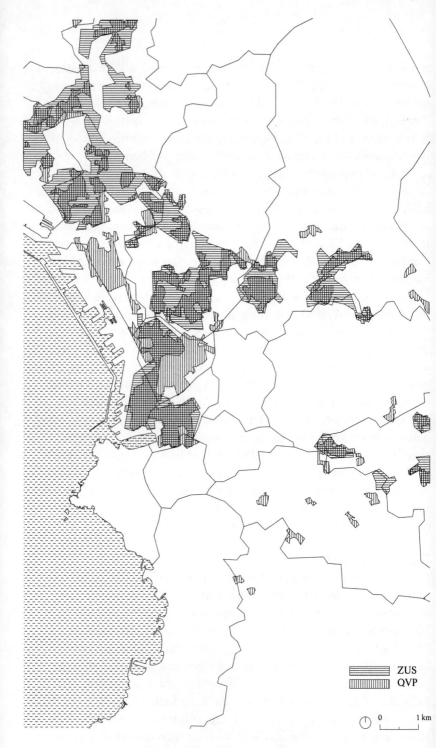

ZUS (*zone urbaine sensible*) and
QPV (*quartier prioritaire de la politique de la ville*)

up to tackle poverty and unemployment, and became a cornerstone of indirect immigration-targeted policies, emerging from French republican universalism in which all citizens are equal regardless of their social, cultural, or political background. Today, while the number of ZUS have decreased nationally, in Marseille and its region the ZUS population has increased, and 18.3 percent of the city's entire population resides in one.[13]

In October 1995, a new urban renewal project called Euroméditerranée, located on and around the harbor area, was initiated and funded by the French central government, the municipality, the department, and the region (later the urban community of Marseille Provence Métropole). Capitalizing on the postindustrial urban fabric, its main purpose was to attract investments and remove lay the basis for a new service-oriented urban economy. Declared of "national interest" in the Opérations d'Intérêt National (OIN), the 310-hectare project was extended in 2007 beyond its original perimeter to become Euroméd II and include an additional 170 hectares. The contested renovation of the Haussmann-style Rue de la République is paradigmatic of the conflict of interests between locals and decision-makers. A poor neighborhood adjacent to the harbor and Le Panier, Rue de la République was home to modest populations— many of them freshly immigrated. With public policies aiming to bring in wealthier populations, inhabitants were expelled and were not able to relocate in the city center. Meanwhile, apartments and shops remain empty as the anticipated population stays away, pointing to a miscalculation of Marseille's economic situation, somehow a limitation to gentrification.

The second phase of Euroméditerranée is an even more blatant speculative real estate scheme, with new construction on a budget and maximum profit as a goal. As the project moves north, the scale of construction increases with the completion of the Ilôt Allard, a.k.a. Smartseille, a 24,000 m² so-called connected-ecological project with 385 housing units—including 100 for social housing. Meanwhile across the street, for the ancient village of Les Crottes, home to a wild mix of newcomers and an impoverished local population, the developer foresees housing, the transformation of the *marché aux puces* via the enormous Les Fabriques project and the extension of the tramway. This only means inhabitants will be compensated and expelled, exemplifying Euroméd as an exclusion machine. This parallel account of migration, housing, and state policies attempts to uncover spatial

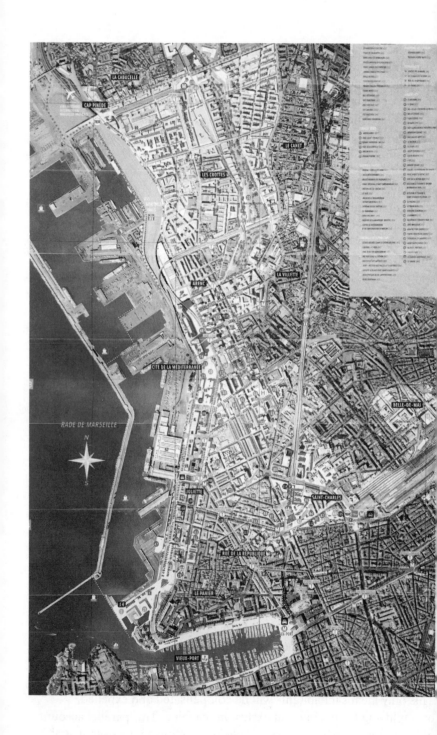

Perimeter of Euroméditerranée

economies within neoliberal logic, demonstrating how the social landscape of the city is deeply intertwined with the housing situation, and results in a consolidated unjust situation between north and south, poor and wealthy, and resource-rich and deprived areas.

1 An in-depth research of the history of immigration in Marseille has been elaborated in the following texts. See the series by Emile Temime, *Migrance: Histoire des migrations à Marseille* (Aix-en-Provence: Edisud): vol. 1 (with Pierre Echinard), *La préhistoire de la migration, 1482–1830* (1989); vol. 2 (with Renée Lopez), *L'expansion marseillaise et l'invasion italienne, 1830–1918* (1990); vol. 3 (with Marie-Françoise Attard-Maraninchi), *Le cosmopolitisme de l'entre-deux-guerres, 1919–1945* (1990); vol. 4 (with Jean-Jacques Jordi and Abdelmalek Sayad), *Le choc de la décolonisation, 1945–1990* (1991; repr., Marseille: Jeanne Lafitte, 2007).

2 Nicole Wiseman, "The Construction of Marseille and the Racialized Immigrant," Academia, 2015, https://www.academia.edu/11575136/.

3 Marcel Maussen, "Guest Workers and Islam in France," chap. 6 of "Constructing Mosques: The Governance of Islam in France and the Netherlands" (PhD diss., UVA University Amsterdam, 2009), https://hdl.handle.net/11245/1.311584.

4 In this way the social structure of Italian or Corsican villages was replicated. Other communities were established around Catholic parishes of Marseille.

5 The residents had a small room for themselves and they could use common spaces such as a kitchen, dining room, and sanitary facilities. They were also subjected to strict discipline: they could not receive female visitors or distribute political pamphlets, and staff could enter their rooms at any moment.

6 The most striking example in Marseille is La Rouvière. This residential complex was built by a private company in order to host hundreds of *pieds-noirs* families. With 2,200 apartments, it is the second biggest co-owned property in France.

7 A striking case of "permanent" *cité de transit* is the Cité Bassens in Marseille. Built in 1963, over the years it became a symbol of segregation, criminality, and urban decay. It was partially demolished almost forty years later after its population was relocated.

8 An emblematic figure that impersonates the political misconduct of this time was Gaston Defferre, Marseille's mayor from 1953 until his death in 1986. Defferre managed to keep his position for thirty years by dividing power between the socialists and the liberal right. He gave socialists power over municipal services and city planning to the liberal right. See Philippe Pujol, La fabrique du monstre: 10 ans d'immersion dans les quartiers nord de Marseille, aa zone la plus pauvre d'Europe *(Paris: Les Arènes, 2015).*

9 Michel Peraldi, Claire Duport, and Michel Samson, *Sociologie de Marseille* (Paris: La Découverte, 2015).

10 Elizabeth Joy Shackney, "Social Mix or Maquillage? Institutions, Immigration, and Integration in Marseille" (MA thesis, Wesleyan University, 2017).

11 After 2007, the Pacte de Reliance Sociale was substituted by another contract called Contrats Urbains de Cohésion Sociale (CUCS), defined by an interministerial committee in March 2006.

12 *Zones urbaines sensibles* (ZUS) were defined by the presence of large complexes and/or degraded neighborhoods characterized by an imbalance between numbers of housing and employment. *Zones de redynamisation urbaine* (ZRU) were characterized by high unemployment rates, large proportions of nongraduates, and low tax potentials. *Zones franches urbaines* (ZFU) have been instituted to favor employment in these areas by giving fiscal exemptions and incentives to companies that decide to set up there. Moreover, ZRU and ZFU are subcategories of the ZUS. In 2015, this categorization was suppressed and substituted by *quartier prioritaire de la politique de la ville* (QPV).

13 Institut national de la statistique et des études économiques, *Populations communales 2006 en ZUS: Recensement de la population*, ed. Insee (Asnières-sur-Seine: 2006).

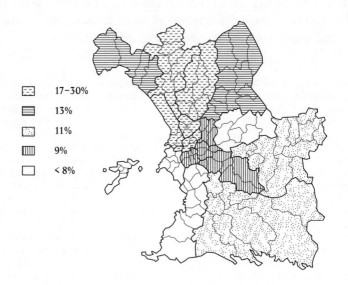

	17–30%
	13%
	11%
	9%
	< 8%

Immigrant population

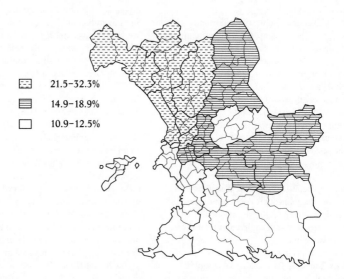

	21.5–32.3%
	14.9–18.9%
	10.9–12.5%

Unemployed population

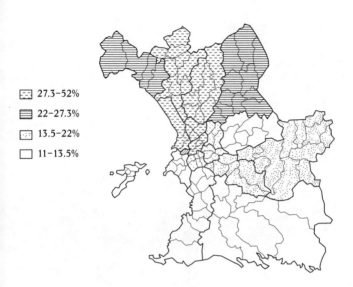

Population under poverty line

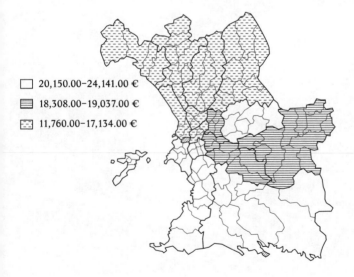

Median disposable income per household

Institut national de la statistique et des études économiques,
Recensement général de la population (2013).

J. Mézard, Minister of Territorial Cohesion and J. Denormandie, Minister Attached to the Minister of Territorial Cohesion:

"The three pillars of the government's housing strategy:
Pillar 1: build more, better and cheaper housing to trigger a 'supply shock.'
Pillar 2: meet the needs of every individual and protect the most vulnerable.
Pillar 3: improve living conditions." [1]

B. L. Mireur, member of Centre ville pour tous:

"Forty thousand apartments in Marseille have been declared indecent housing (*copropriétés dégradées*) in an old registry that, together with the poverty indicator threshold, is guiding statistically based policies. According to the current regulations, all dwellings should be decent, should guarantee sanitary safety and structural security. The responsibility is with the state. In Marseille they force the owners to take care of the maintenance. However, after the security measures have been taken, usually people go back to their houses and realize that just a part of the problem has been solved. People feel very insecure and there is a lack of trust in the public actors." [2]

1   Mézard, J. *The Government's Housing Strategy: Jacques Mézard, Minister of Territorial Cohesion and Julien Denormandie, Minister of State Attached to the Minister of Territorial Cohesion, Presented the Government's "Housing" Strategy on 20 September 2017.*, 2017.

2   B. L. Mireur, interview by MAS Urban Design, Marseille, France, March 19, 2019.

GRANDS ENSEMBLES: DOMESTIC SOLUTION, COLLECTIVE PROBLEM

Early Housing Solutions (1930s–1950s)

In the aftermath of World War II and its massive destruction, housing became a critical issue. The rapid population growth and subsequent housing shortages initiated a major shift in the French government's reconstruction policies. The state began to promote mass production of publicly funded housing, especially on the outskirts of existing cities, resulting in what could be described as a postwar urbanization frenzy.[1] This unprecedented public involvement in social housing can be credited to a general change of mentality. As scholar Kenny Cupers explains, "Architecture undertook a whole new role—a social project. In those years modern architecture did not belong solely to an avant-garde; it was shared and shaped by government officials, construction companies, residents associations, real estate developers and social scientists alike."[2] The rhetoric surrounding these projects was largely consistent and signals an effort for universal access to housing and public services, regardless of social background. Radical changes came about not only with new building techniques (e.g., prefabricated construction) but also regarding the modus operandi of construction companies and financial groups (i.e., unions, co-operatives).[3] Some of the ideas developed in these projects were not pursued fully, while others became the norm for new cities across France in the form of *grands ensembles*.

Of the four housing precedents presented here, it should come as no surprise that those aimed at housing middle-income classes (Unité d'Habitation, SOGIMA) are in the southern area of Marseille, while the ones targeting lower-income classes are located in the northern districts (Saint-Barthelemy, Saint-Just), where 60 percent of the city's social housing will emerge and various migrant populations settled in the subsequent decades.[4]

EARLY HOUSING SOLUTIONS

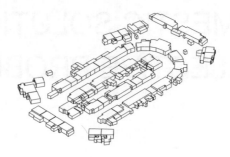

Cité-jardin Saint-Just, 1931, J. Lajarrige, B. Lariche, L. Poutu, E. Senes, 148 apartments
District 3 (13003), Avenue Lucien Allonge, Marseille

Commissioned by the municipality in the frame of the *habitations bon marché* (HBM) program, this garden city (*cité-jardin*) was designed for middle-income groups. It presents single adjoining houses with four units on the ground floor and buildings with two units on the upper floor. They have a simple layout and design language, homogeneous facade, and material palette typical of the "pavilion-style."

Somewhat contained, the complex was served by a school, a bakery, and grocery stores. Today, extensions and additions have been built in the private gardens. The current public owner, Habitat Marseille Provence, wishes to get rid of this aging and unprofitable estate, and tenants of one of the oldest garden cities (with Chutes-Lavie, Saint-Louis, Haute-Rive) are offered the opportunity to buy their units.[5]

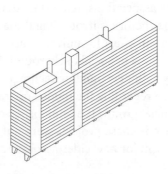

Unité d'Habitation, 1947–1952, Le Corbusier, 337 apartments
District 8 (13008), Boulevard Michelet, Marseille

Promoted as a response to the postwar housing demand, this state-funded architectural icon marked a radical break in the use of concrete and became a reference for housing interventions for decades. Eighteen floors high, it houses 1,200 residents in private apartments,

along with a shared communal floor, shops, working spaces, and a hotel-restaurant. Some experts consider this building as indirectly forestalling and inspiring the *grands ensembles* typologies: the lone-standing unit has also been presented as an anti-city model.[6]

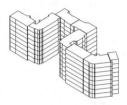

SOGIMA-Périer, immeubles à loyers moyens, 1937–1938, C. Favel, L.-C. Heckly, 120 apartments
District 8 (13008), Boulevard Gaston Crémieux, Marseille

After working in Paris, architect Louis-Clovis Heckly designed a Bauhaus-style residential building for the middle class within the bourgeois neighborhoods in Marseille. It was built on behalf of the Société de Gestion Immobilière de la Ville de Marseille (SOGIMA) and Société Nouvelle de Travaux Urbains. The architectural and decorative elements, such as an open courtyard and art nouveau–inspired details, were designed to appeal to the targeted populations' aesthetics.[7]

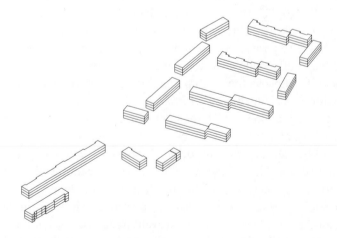

Ensemble Saint-Barthelemy, 1953, C. Lestrade, 200 apartments
District 14 (13014), Chemin de Sainte-Marthe, Marseille

A low-rise, high-density, linear housing project with a few shops on the ground floor, this complex was planned as a village for employees of the national train company Société Nationale des Chemins de fer Français (SNCF). A modular repetition of units in a simple structural grid allowed for fast and cheap construction and the creation of open spaces, creating a pleasant rural atmosphere.[8]

Grands Ensembles and Demolition Policies

The term *grand ensemble* was used for the first time in 1935 to describe La Muette, a *cité* in Drancy at the gates of Paris. This neologism, and the term *cité*, refer to a specific urban form that became popular in postwar France as a solution to the acute housing crisis.[9] Postwar reconstruction was seen as an opportunity to rebuild French cities according to modern principles that would eventually create a more just social order.[10] Two groups of actors were responsible for this domestic revolution: on the one hand, officials of the Ministry for Reconstruction and Urbanization (Ministère de la Reconstruction et de l'Urbanisme), and on the other, architects from the modern movement which, together, sought to mobilize new design, materials, and construction techniques to reframe the relationship between housing and the urban fabric. Large-scale prefabricated concrete housing projects were hence the result of a civic mission intended to guarantee high standards of living to the whole population regardless of social class. Perhaps it is important to mention that these thousands of new public apartments, *habitation à loyer modéré* (HLM), were not to house the poor or the immigrant population, but were simply considered the most efficient response to the national housing crisis. Their decline started in the 1970s, when the most affluent families vacated the HLM stock to access homeownership. Slowly, these residential complexes became home to poorer populations marginalized by the labor market and unable to afford the costs to maintain the property.

Policies to improve these dilapidated suburbs were devised in the 1990s with the agenda known as Politique de la Ville. Based on a set of socioeconomic tools, which included citizens' participation, for local improvements and grassroots investments, its success was limited. At the turn of the century, the authorities decreased funding for these community-centered mechanisms of urban regeneration and instead instituted new policies that relied on territorial remodeling as a tool to solve social problems—and to satisfy construction lobbies. In 2003, the Borloo Law explicitly aimed at preventing the consolidation of ghettos and at facilitating social cohesion in the *zones urbaines sensibles (ZUS)*, previously defined by the Politique de la Ville.[11] Operatively, this ordinance established the national agency for urban renewal, Agence Nationale pour la Rénovation Urbaine (ANRU), which administers the implementation and financing of the national urban renewal program (Programme National pour la Rénovation Urbaine). The great novelty of this institutional framework, compared to past administrative practices, is that it relies heavily on demolitions. Authorities argue that this mechanism can change the image of these neighborhoods and destigmatize its inhabitants. In practice, they are in fact providing opportunities toward some form of gentrification and expanding the private property market, while sending a critical message to current occupants.[12]

These vicissitudes show the limits of two different and yet similar spatial approaches to socio-urban issues. On the one hand, the modernist dream of the *grands ensembles*, temporarily credited for solving the housing crisis, is the physical base for the creation of large-scale ghettos, linked to design decisions of mass, location, and size. On the other hand, the new demolition policy—which shares with the modernist estates the "grand gesture approach"—is simply a mechanism to literally remove the social problem and provide more space for speculation.[13]

Degraded Co-ownerships (*copropriétés dégradées*): A Matter of National Interest

A misunderstanding often occurs regarding the ownership status of the *grands ensembles*, which can be wrongly perceived as purely social and public housing. This is not always the case. *Grands ensembles* occur in the city in the form of privately owned condominiums (*copropriétés,* or co-ownerships). A co-ownership is basically any building divided into multiple individual properties, containing rights over one housing unit and part of the building's common elements (i.e., facade, roof, common spaces).[14] The first legal framework defining co-ownerships in France was formed in 1936, when this new type of collective ownership was quickly spreading and common legal guidelines became indispensable.[15] Initially, co-ownership laws sought to safeguard both collective benefit and the rights of co-owners, but later adaptations and additions increasingly facilitated the interference of external and public bodies after "condominiums in difficulty" (*copropriétés en difficulté*), or "degraded co-ownerships," started appearing in the mid-1990s.[16] These are unmaintained, decaying housing estates, with a high concentration of underprivileged populations.[17]

There are several reasons why a *grand ensemble* would become a deteriorated condominium.[18] Residents typically belong to the poor working class, the most vulnerable stratum of society. According to scholar Olivier Schwartz, what defines the working class is "a low professional or social status, limited economic resources—without necessarily meaning precariousness—and the distance to cultural capital, and [...] school."[19] Additionally, as pointed out by Johanna Lees, these spaces became home to another specific category of the population: people in a migratory, transitory state.[20] Thus, residents of these large co-ownerships are working class, frequently foreigners or people who have acquired French nationality. Kenny Cupers argues unambiguously that "as white middle-class families left collective housing in favor of suburban single-family homes, they were replaced by poor families, many from North Africa and sub-Saharan Africa."[21] Paradoxically, maintenance costs charged to the owners of these grands ensembles are extremely high, as much as 400 euros per month, while the most basic services are no longer provided. This is because the co-ownership has accumulated debt and is no longer able to pay for suppliers and service providers. Dissatisfied with the lack of maintenance, owners refuse to pay, and the co-ownership debt rises exponentially.

City efforts to solve degraded co-ownerships intensified during the 1990s and have largely resorted to rehabilitation processes and demolitions. When an estate is found in extreme dereliction and its rehabilitation exceeds the city's means, it can be declared by the state as an intervention of national interest (OIN), at which point a betterment program is launched (Opérations de Requalification des Copropriétés Dégradées, ORCOD).[22] On extreme sites which have already undergone several phases of rehabilitation, state-led rescue plans *(plans de sauvegarde)* mainly focus on formal aspects rather than problematic social aspects, contributing to a questionable stigmatization of the urban form. With demolitions and evictions as their main tools, the real issue of poverty and social inequality is simply deflected rather than addressed.[23]

1 Kenny Cupers, "The Social Project," Places Journal, April 2014. Accessed 14 Jul 2020. https://doi.org/10.22269/140402

2 Ibid.

3 Marie-Jeanne Dumont, Le logement social à Paris, 1850–1930: Les habitations à bon marché (Liège: Mardaga, 1991).

4 Emile Témime and Pierre Echinard, Migrance: Histoire des migrations a Marseille, vol. 4 (Aix-en-Provence: Edisud, 1991).

5 Musée virtuel du logement social, "La cité jardin Saint-Just, à Marseille," Les HLM en Expos, accessed August 6, 2019, http://musee-hlm.fr/ark:/naan /a011507798835fOC2fb.

6 Philippe Panerai, Jean Castex, and Jean-Charles Depaule, Formes urbaines: De l'îlot à la barre (Paris: Dunod, 1978).

7 Jean-Louis Cohen and André Lortie, Des fortifs au périf: Paris, les seuils de la ville (Paris: Picard éditeur, 2000).

8 Thierry Durousseau, Ensembles et résidences à Marseille, 1955–1975 (Marseille: Bik et Book, 2009).

9 Maurice Rotival, "Les grands ensembles," L'Architecture d'Aujourd'hui 1, no. 6 (June 1935): 57–72.

10 Nicole C. Rudolph, At Home in Postwar France: Modern Mass Housing and the Right to Comfort (New York: Berghahn Books, 2015).

11 Loi n° 2003-710 du 1er août 2003 d'orientation et de programmation pour la ville et la rénovation urbaine.

12 Agnès Deboulet and Simone Abram, "Are Social Mix and Participation Compatible? Conflicts and Claims in Urban Renewal in France and England," in Social Housing and Urban Renewal, ed. Paul Watt and Peer Smets (Emerald Publishing Limited, 2017), 141–77, https://doi.org/

13 Elisa Bertagnini, "The French Banlieues between Appropriation and Demolition," Planum: The Journal of Urbanism 2, no. 27 (October 2013), http://www.planum.net /download/living-landscapes-conference -bertagnini-section-7.

14 The size of each part or portion of the property depends on the area, condition, and value of the private property, and can include corridors, elevators, common terraces, gardens, and so forth.

15 Sébastien Vincent, "L'intervention sur les copropriétés dégradées dans les programmes de renouvellement urbain" (MA thesis, Institut d'Urbanisme et d'Aménagement Régional d'Aix-en-Provence, 2017), https://dumas.ccsd.cnrs .fr/dumas-01616386/document.

16 These are different from most co-ownerships built before 1949, which are located in the city center and are usually inhabited by elderly people.

17 Sylvaine Le Garrec, "Les copropriétés en difficulté dans les grands ensembles: Le cas de Clichy-Montfermeil," Espaces et sociétés 156–57, no. 1 (January 2014): 53–68.

18 Agnès Berland-Berthon, "Les grands ensembles: Des quartiers pas comme les autres," in Pérennité urbaine, ou la ville par-delà ses métamorphoses, vol. 2, Turbulences, ed. Colette Vallat (Paris: L'Harmattan, 2007), 255–68.

19 Olivier Schwartz, "Peut-on parler des classes populaires?," La vie des idées, September 13, 2011, https://laviedesidees .fr/Peut-on-parler-des-classes.html.

20 Johanna Lees, "Les copropriétés dégradées de l'après-guerre à Marseille: Un nouvel habitat social de fait," Espaces et sociétés 156–57, no. 1 (January 2014): 69–84, doi:10.3917/esp.156.0069.

21 Kenny Cupers, "The Social Project," Places Journal, April 2014. Accessed 14 Jul 2020. https://doi.org/10.22269/140402

22 This includes property acquisitions, construction works, and relocation of the previous residents. See Vincent, "L'intervention sur les copropriétés dégradées."

23 Ibid.

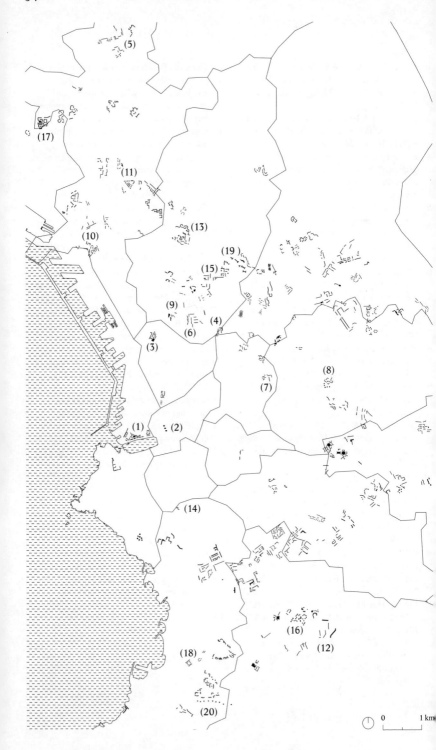

Marseille's *grands ensembles*

GRANDS ENSEMBLES IN MARSEILLE 1950s–1970s

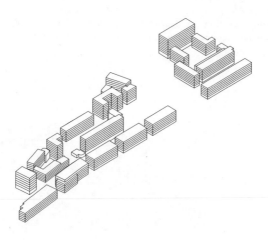

(1) Vieux Port & La Tourette, 1948–1955, F. Pouillon, 260 apartments
District 2 (13002), Vieux Port, Marseille

The projects of La Tourette and Vieux Port are indicative of Fernand Pouillon's design principles. The contained order of the spatial arrangements into comprehensive *ensembles*, the intricate materiality of the buildings, as well as their financial and construction efficiency highlight Pouillon's preoccupation with formal, cultural, and historical continuity. Through the repetition of both building types and floor plans, mass housing was made available for private ownership.[1]

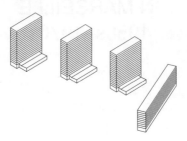

(2) La Bourse, 1954, R. Boileau, J.-H. Labourdette, 310 apartments
District 1 (13001), Cours Belsunce, Marseille

On an area that remained vacant for decades following the expropriation of residents and the demolition of substandard housing from the Bourse district in 1911, the Labourdette agency was selected to design 500 housing units with underground parking and a shopping center. Due to the discovery of the old port's Phoenician archaeological vestiges, the project was only partially realized and 310 units were built. The exoskeleton structure of reinforced concrete allows for a high flexibility of occupancy.[2]

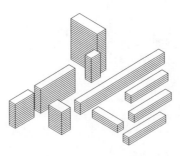

(3) Parc Bellevue (a.k.a. Félix Pyat), 1954, R. Egger, 814 apartments
District 3 (13003), Rue Félix Pyat, Marseille

The Félix Pyat project was inaugurated in 1954 and is composed of several blocks in a modernist postwar style of towers and low-rise longitudinal buildings. Built in response to the postwar housing crises, through the years it typically housed people with migrant backgrounds. The complex deteriorated over the years and underwent several renovations and demolition campaigns.[3]

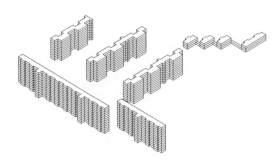

(4) Les Rosiers, 1954–1957, J. Rozan, 752 apartments
District 14 (13014), Residence Les Rosiers, Marseille

Les Rosiers provides extraordinary complex vertical and horizontal circulation, which forms an engaging architectural promenade. The buildings are organized as an overlay of rows of three- or four-story blocks with cellars below and apartments above. Each block is separated by a row of cellars that open onto a wide corridor, also called "platforms" by the residents. Elevators stop every second floor, where the platforms are located.[4] The complex is predominantly inhabited by Comorian immigrants.

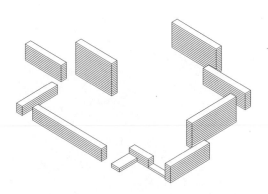

(5) Parc Kallistè, 1955, C. Gros, A. H. de Vallaurie, S. Woods, C. Giampietri, 752 apartments
District 15 (13015), Chemin des Bourrelys, Marseille

Inspired by modernist urbanism, the design was intended to liberate the ground, allowing for large parks while achieving maximum sunlight and fresh air. Facades and plans are characterized by uniformity and narrow slabs (10.5 meters wide). The all-concrete construction with prefabricated facade elements is in poor condition, with some of the buildings left vacant, open to squatters and finally secured in anticipation of demolition.[5]

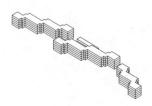

(6) Super Belvédère, 1955, G. Candilis, A. Josic, S. Woods, C. Giampietri, 160 apartments
District 14 (13014), Rue Louis Merlino, Marseille

The winning entry of a competition held in 1954, Super Belvédère is a housing complex consisting of 160 units for residents from the middle-to-low income class. The architects proposed circulation with minimum wasted exterior and interior space, proper ventilation, natural lighting, and views of the surrounding environment. It is a successful, rather well-maintained example of modern architecture.[6]

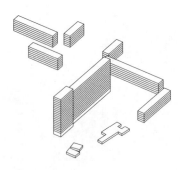

(7) Résidence Beausoleil, 1957–1960, A. Devin, 450 apartments
District 12 (13012), Boulevard de Roux, Marseille

Based on the idea of the cité radieuse, the Résidence Beausoleil project was built by the Société Civile Immobilière Beausoleil. It was part of a broader urban program that included sports areas and schools, facilities which hadn't been constructed. The main high-rise contrasts with the low height of the other six buildings. While the project offers interesting answers to the mass housing issue, the buildings' ground floor and public spaces aren't well solved.[7]

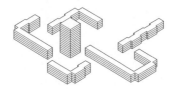

(8) Les Lierres, 1958–1967, P. Averous, M. Scialom, 312 apartments
District 12 (13012), Avenue du 24 Avril, Marseille

This complex is composed of five low-rise buildings and a sixteen-story tower that create an enclosed block with public spaces and parking in the center. Apartments range between 45 and 90 m² with two to four rooms. The structure and facade are designed in a grid of prefabricated elements, which made for affordable and efficient construction. The residents are also provided with shared laundries, common rooms, and sports facilities.[8]

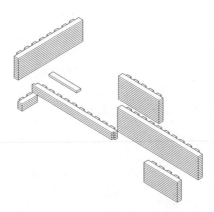

(9) Ensemble La Marine Bleue, 1959, E. Castel, A. Devin, E. Gautier, J. Rozan & J. Sourdeau, 788 apartments, District 14 (13014), Groupe La Marine Bleue, Marseille

Part of the national industrialized program for low-rent housing (HLM), La Marine Bleue consists of six buildings characterized by prefabricated elements, prioritizing financial and construction efficiency. The typical floor plan is repeated and each staircase serves three apartments per floor. The modules of the facade are 5.4 m high (accommodating two floors) and 0.6 m thick and differentiated by the use of various patterns.[9]

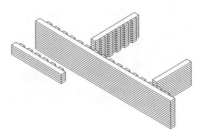

(10) Campagne Lévêque, 1959, J. Rozan, R. Egger, L. Poutu, L. Olmeta, 800 apartments
District 16 (13016), Avenue de Saint-Louis, Marseille

Part of the HLM initiative to provide standardized housing, which formed Campagne Lévêque, an eighteen-month mortgage period was set up to comply with the new low-cost rental policy. This monumental bar is 40 m high and 275 m long. It was the longest housing block in Europe when constructed. The neighborhood is completed by a college, a primary school, and a social center.[10]

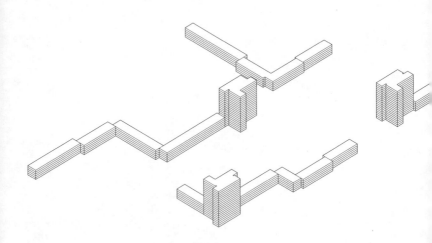

(11) La Viste, 1959–1965, G. Candilis, A. Josic, S. Woods, P. Dony, 703 apartments
District 15 (13015), Route de la Viste, Marseille

Winning an architectural competition, the renowned team proposed for La Viste a set of apartment buildings on an orthogonal grid, a rhythm of low buildings and towers of more than eighteen floors. The use of pure prisms, smooth facades, and colors brings unique aesthetics to the recently renovated project.[11]

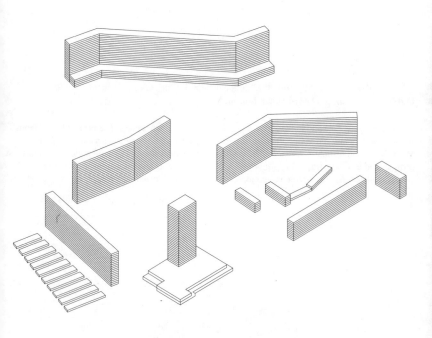

(12) La Rouvière, 1961–1971, R. Guyot, 2,200 apartments
District 9 (13009), Boulevard du Redon, Marseille

The monumental scale of La Rouvière makes it a striking element in the city's skyline. It was designed in the 1960s to host Algerian returnees and is still the largest co-ownership in Europe. The estate is accessed by a single road that serves seven buildings; due to its remoteness up on the hills it is self-sustaining in many ways, with schools, a shopping center, and cultural centers, all built with modern construction techniques and a landscaped park.[12]

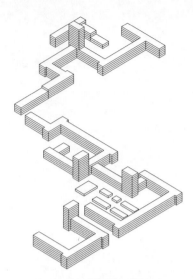

(13) Parc Maurelette, 1962–1964, E. Chirié, P. Chirié, J. Chirié, 745 apartments
District 15 (13015), Boulevard Simon Bolivar, Marseille

Despite using average and inexpensive construction means and materials, Parc Maurelette is no ordinary *ensemble*. The estate is organized around a traditional square, streets, and ramparts as a reinterpretation of historical tendencies. The project harmoniously articulates housing and services, landscape and construction. High unemployment rates of residents and poor transportation to the city center plague the complex.[13]

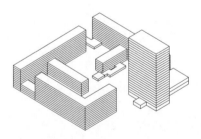

(14) Le Méditerranée, 1962–1973, Atelier 9, 547 apartments
District 6 (13006), Avenue de Toulon, Marseille

Le Méditerranée follows the concept of an "open island" integrating mixed habitats, offices, and shops in blocks open to the city. It offers a wide range of apartments with balconies overlooking a central yard. The project was intended for the upper middle class, which subsequently left for residences on the city's periphery. It is currently populated by residents with more modest means. The project benefits from its ideal central location and is relatively well maintained.[14]

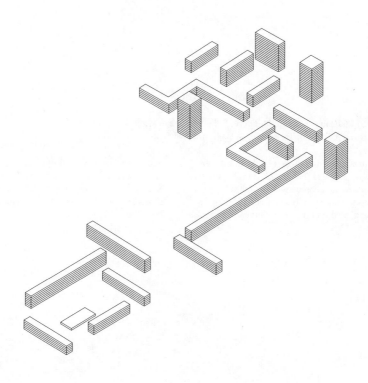

(15) Picon Busserine, 1964–1969, F. Madeline, A. Bondon, C. Lestrade, P. Averous, M. Scialom, 1,528 apartments, District 14 (13014), Rue Font Vert, Marseille

Picon Busserine was built in 1947 after an architectural competition for new neighborhoods intended to reduce slums built on the area at the time. The project was an opportunity for innovations in civil engineering and architecture to advance existing building construction efficiency, costs, and techniques.[15]

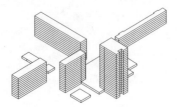

(16) Château Sec, 1966, M. Fabre, B. Laville, 512 apartments
District 9 (13009), Traverse de la Gaye, Marseille

Château Sec is a project by the developer George Laville (father of B. Laville) and his construction company. The architects' goal was to combine efficiency and diversity to avoid a "dormitory city." Served by schools and a social center, and by public services such as a library, a shopping center, and a sport's field, it proves that certain solutions can solve short-term problems while withstanding the test of time.[16]

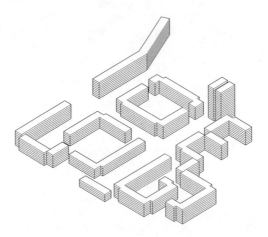

(17) La Castellane, 1966–1969, F. Boukobza, P. Jameux, P. Mathoulin, P. Meillassoux, 1,249 apartments, District 15 (13015), Boulevard Barnier, Marseille

A modernist council estate built in the 1960s, La Castellane is now home to about 7,000 residents, largely from North Africa. Units were repeated across the project with the prefabrication technique Tracoba, resulting in a homogeneous facade pattern. The neighborhood suffers from high rates of unemployment and poverty.[17]

(18) Les Petites Résidences, 1969, A. Bondon, 220 apartments
District 8 (13008), Rue Dr Bertrand, Marseille

Les Petites Résidences is situated close to the sea. Its presence gave the area a residential character since it introduced the concept of the residential block. Although it includes a handful of relatively tall structures, the project maintains a human scale since the design approach harmonizes urban gardens and domestic structures by hybridizing the modernist grid with the freestanding villa.[18]

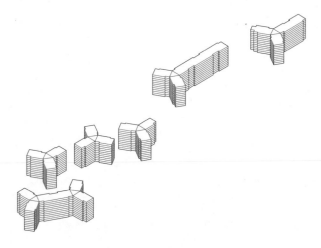

(19) Les Flamants, 1972, J. Carrot, C. Delfante, P. Jameux, B. Laville, 403 apartments
District 14 (13014), Chemin de Sainte-Marthe, Marseille

The complex Les Flamants presents an original assembly in the form of a three-pronged star without central circulation. The typical pre-fabricated system of mass housing is repeated in other complexes, offering a combination of variously sized apartments. So far, the complex has undergone two moderately successful rehabilitations that are symptomatic of the problematic handover of these renovations to private companies.[19]

(20) Parc du Roy d'Espagne, 1975, G. Gillet, L. Olmeta, 1678 apartments
District 8 (13008), Allée Emmanuel Chabrier, Marseille

The complex is located in the southern hills of Marseille and draws from Alvar Aalto's concept of a "forest town." Small-scale apartment blocks organized around patios and ten residential towers cohabitate within a green landscape. Despite its density, its mass is scattered along the topography and only the towers emerge from the greenery. Its location on the edge of the city makes the complex difficult to reach without a car, a clear sign of social segregation.[20]

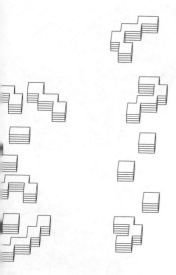

1 Francesca Patrono, Mirko Russo, Claudia Sansú, and Fernand Pouillon. *Fernand Pouillon: Costruzione, Città, Paesaggio*, (Naeples: CLEAN edizioni, 2018).

2 Thierry Durousseau, "Notices monographiques des 80 ensembles et résidences étudiés," in *Marseille, ensembles et résidences de la période 1955/1975*, ed. Ministère de la Culture (Marseille: Drac Provence-Alpes-Côte d'Azur, 2020).

3 Jean-Christophe Nourisson, *Parc Bellevue XXe siècle: Une oeuvre pour le quartier Saint-Mauront à Marseille* (Paris: Sens & Tonka, 1995).

4 Durousseau, "Notices monographiques des 80 ensembles et résidences étudiés."

5 "Parc Kallisté," Marseille Rénovation Urbaine, accessed August 8, 2019, http://www.marseille-renovation-urbaine.fr/kalliste/parc-kalliste-234.

6 Durousseau, "Notices monographiques des 80 ensembles et résidences étudiés."

7 Ibid.

8 Ibid.

9 Ibid.

10 Ibid.

11 Ibid.

12 Thierry Durousseau, *Ensembles et résidences à Marseille, 1955–1975* (Marseille: Bik et Book, 2009).

13 Thierry Durousseau, "Notices monographiques des 80 ensembles et résidences étudiés"

14 Durousseau, "Notices monographiques des 80 ensembles et résidences étudiés."

15 Ibid.

16 Ibid.

17 Ibid.

18 Ibid.

19 Ibid.

20 Ibid.

MARSEILLE, THE GREAT MOVE

1945–1975

Thierry Durousseau

Fueled by years of colonization, Marseille underwent a tentative modernization of both the port and the city at the turn of the twentieth century. After the deadly fire of the Nouvelles Galeries department store in 1938, the municipality remained under state supervision (*sous–tutelle*) when war broke out. The city experienced firsthand the loss of the finest European intellects, from Walter Benjamin to Hannah Arendt, as they fled fascism. Despite its distance from the battlefields, Marseille was nevertheless bombed by Italian, German, and American forces. In February 1942, the German army, under Hitler's direct injunction, undertook the systematic destruction of the districts of the old city. At the end of the war, the city was reduced to 550,000 inhabitants, with 20,000 buildings destroyed. Reconstruction began in 1949 with Georges Meyer-Heine's master plan, produced jointly by the municipality and the state. This plan remained in force until the creation of the Plan d'Occupation des Sols (Land-Use Plan, POS) in 1974.

  Reconstruction efforts included two exceptional projects: rebuilding the port districts, which mobilized the majority of local architects, and construction of the Le Corbusier housing block, the Cité Radieuse, outside the city and exempted from regulatory contingencies. However distant these might be, both projects refer to a sublimated Mediterranean tradition. Le Corbusier generalizes the garden cell or loggia with its sunshade, it organizes a facade pleated with drop shadows that show textured or perforated concrete. At the port, André Leconte rejects bow windows in favor of loggias. Fernand Pouillon's *coup de force* on the harbor front consists in doubling the facades with deep loggias framed by solid stone pillars, which owed as much to the Corbusian villas as to Frank Lloyd Wright's shade drawings. Elsewhere, he uses the ceramic screens of Frédéric and Philippe Sourdive or turns wooden grills into *moucharabieh* balconies, light traps that André-Jacques Dunoyer de Segonzac refers to as "Brazilian architecture."

Housing, housing, and more housing! In Marseille, as in the whole of France, this was the central motto. Housing shortage became a pressing matter as the population increased from 636,000 inhabitants in 1954 to 908,000 inhabitants in 1975, with French returnees arriving from North Africa—a figure never to be exceeded again. The major task for authorities and architects, housing materialized by slabs and towers, forms from then on prevalent in the Marseille landscape in a wide variety of production and authorship. The architects' generation trained before the war took control: André Devin, Yvan Bentz, Louis Olmeta. All demonstrated an urban and temperate modernity toward new standards. Jean Rozan deployed a spatial language at the roots of modern architecture; Dunoyer de Segonzac systematically employed raw concrete. To catch up with the sudden urban growth, the municipality of Marseille commissioned numerous schools, allowing for René Egger and Fernand Pouillon to develop a school model that rationalizes the use of resources, using local means (i.e., methods, labor force, materials, and tools) for a suitable architecture with regional character.

Collective housing programs became more specific, in particular in terms of size, and at the advent of the Fifth Republic in 1958, the housing estates comprised between 300 and 800 units each. To avoid the failure of dormitory cities, the Société Centrale Immobilière de la Caisse des Dépôts (SCIC, the financial arm of the state) oversaw the construction of estates that combined housing, equipment, and facilities. In 1958, André Devin, Jean-Louis Sourdeau, and Maurice Cialom delivered the 390 housing units of Campagne Larousse, in Le Canet (14th district), for which André Arbus designed the outdoor spaces. The first Cité Universitaire Gaston Berger (400 rooms, 1960, 1st district), near the main train station Saint-Charles, was built by Jacques Berthelot and Christian Pichoux—and became a referential object. Among the most important local developments,

La Viste (700 housing units, 15th district), built in 1962 by Georges
Candilis, Alexis Josic, and Shadrach Wood in association with Louis
Olmeta, is undoubtedly the most internationally known ensemble
of Marseille after the Cité Radieuse. The same year, also for the
SCIC, the architects of Sarcelles, Roger Boileau and Jacques Henri-
Labourdette, constructed an urban complex of towers overlooking
the Cours Belsunce, the famous "Labourdette towers," behind the
stock exchange (310 housing units, 1st district), on a terrain which has
remained vacant for forty years.

After Algerian independence, Marseille found itself at the center
of a real estate crisis. An architectural model of private residences
close to the *grands ensembles* and social housing emerged. Among the
achievements of this period are La Maurelette (1964, 745 dwellings,
15th district) by Jacques and Pierre Chirié and their father Eugène,
who inaugurated a new form of design where architects, landscape
designers, colorists, and sociologists work together to create a visual
and urban environment based on the model of the neighborhood
cluster. Pierre Aveyrous and Maurice Scialom created a real urban
boundary in Les Lierres (1966, 312 housing units, 12th district).
Bernard Laville and Mario Fabre built Château Sec (1966, 499
dwellings, 9th district), a residence with several towers set above a
raised foundation, following an identical construction system. In 1967,
Fernand Boukobza built Le Brasilia (221 dwellings, 8th district) just
opposite of the Cité Radieuse, without deference to the work of Le
Corbusier but with a tribute-like sculptural staircase. Pierre Jameux,
with Les Platanes (1967, 145 dwellings, 14th district), combined brick
and raw concrete in a virtuoso manner for an estate composed of very
diverse forms: towers, squares, and curved buildings.

Despite these successes, the national media failed to promote
the work of Marseille's architects. The Union of Architects banned
during the war and replaced by the Architects Association (Ordre des
Architectes), created *Prado*, a magazine in which local architects could
publish their projects. Around 1965, several collective organizations
were set up by architects for medium co-operatives, research groups,
or training classes. In 1968, however, students of the School of
Architecture, which had just been completed by René Egger, were
highly critical of the period's architecture and approach, questioning
and undermining the drive for constant development. Nevertheless,
the housing factory remained constant, achieving a rate of 550,000
homes per year in France by the mid-seventies.

This final period is not without its successes in Marseille. Le Mediterranée (1970, 457 dwellings, 6th district) by architects Robert Inglesakis and Georges Lefèvre (Atelier 9) formed an open urban island centered on an office tower. Le Roy d'Espagne (1972, 836 dwellings, 9th district) by Guillaume Gillet and Louis Olmeta, located in a pine forest, combined terrace housing, small blocks on piles, a few buildings, and a shopping center, with towers completing the system. Finally, at the foot of the Saint-Cyr mountain range, Castelroc-le-Haut (1974, 1,029 dwellings, 10th district) by Claude Gros enhanced the spatial dimension of the buildings whose elevators and footbridges improved the architectural promenade. In 1973, the Guichard decree put an end to the construction of large housing estates in France, and with even greater finality the first oil crisis ended urban development. After this great readjustment and focus on the periphery, which characterized the Marseille landscape from crisis to crisis, a new architectural and urban era would be marked by a return toward the city center.

NEIGHBOR-HOODS

1. Belsunce 2. Noailles 3. Félix Pyat 4. Parc Kallisté
5. La Rouvière 6. La Castellane 7. Euroméditerranée II

BELSUNCE

The Arrival Neighborhood

Between Saint-Charles station and the port—major infrastructures of departure and arrival—lies the neighborhood of Belsunce. Emerging in the seventeenth century, the area developed with shops and warehouses popular for trade with both native and foreign residents. Belsunce's urban fabric is dominated by the typical three-windows (trois-fenêtres) typology, a prevalent model largely preserved today. Since the 1980s, Belsunce has been the target of public rehabilitation policies that aim to "restore" a manufactured image of a glorious past, stigmatizing poor populations and migrant communities.[1] Despite these attempts to gentrify the area (i.e., Bibliothéque de l'Alcazar, Hotel de Région), Belsunce remains an efficient arrival neighborhood. One can find shabby but affordable lodging on a daily, monthly, or annual basis as well as informal jobs, perhaps prior to moving elsewhere in the city. Belsunce also absorbs various populations, from settled *chabanis* (retired Algerian workers) living in small hotels to Syrian refugees and provincial students, and can be considered an exemplary case of inclusivity. This model, however, is under threat. As Belsunce is on the fringes of the Euroméditerranée urban renewal project, municipal pressure to remove migrant and foreign populations further to the periphery is ever-present, revealing Marseille's inequalities.[2]

1 Sylvie Mazzella, "Le quartier Belsunce à Marseille: Les immigrés dans les traces de la ville bourgeoise," *Les Annales de la Recherche Urbaine* 72, no. 1 (1996): 119–25, https://doi .org/10.3406/aru.1996.1987.
2 Ludovic Bonduel, "Gentrification Policies and Urban Protests in Marseille," Urban Media Lab, February 11, 2019, http://labgov.city/theurbanmedialab/gentrification-policies-and-urban -protests-in-marseille/.

0   20 m

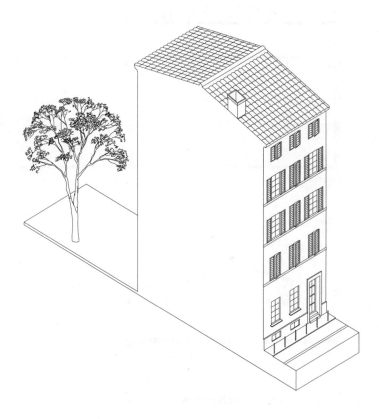

The three-windows (trois-fenêtres) typology—a prevalent model in the neighborhood of Belsunce—appeared in the seventeenth century as an optimized standardization that emerged from speculative urbanization. The plot sizes were fixed at seven meters wide and about thirty meters long, with two buildings at the extremities facing the streets and a courtyard in the middle. Today, the norm is one apartment per floor, with bedrooms facing the street side and living room and kitchen overlooking the backyard. Buildings can have up to seven floors. The use of traditional materials (i.e., tiles) coupled with high ceilings and gardens forms an excellent natural ventilation system that answers to local climatic conditions.

The trois-fenêtres typology

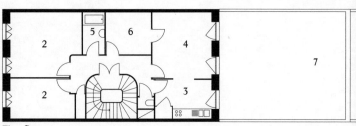

First floor

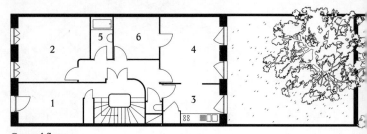

Ground floor

1 Entrance   5 WC bathroom
2 Bedroom   6 Storage room *cafoutch*
3 Kitchen   7 Courtyard
4 Living room

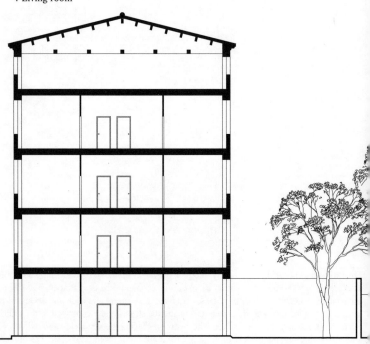

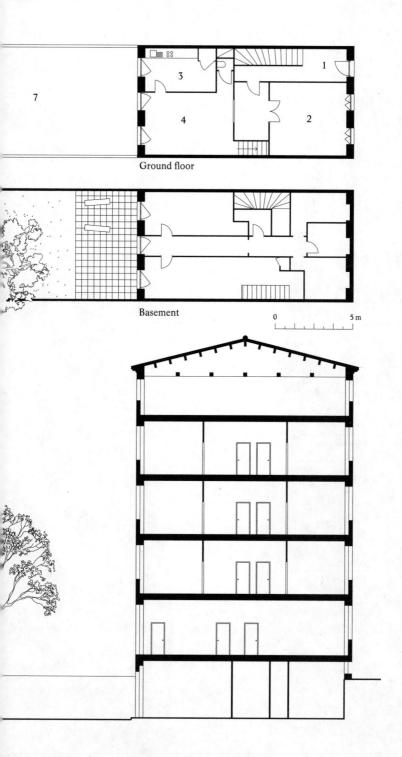

Ground floor

Basement

0   5 m

The trois-fenêtres typology

Métropole Aix-Marseille-Provence:

"A public inquiry procedure happens prior to the implementation of major decisions or the carrying out of certain operations likely to have an impact on the environment. This procedure makes it possible to inform the public about the project and to collect its appreciations or its critics. An independent and impartial investigating commissioner collects the citizens' comments, notably by receiving the public in a local office, and ensures that the public is well informed before the investigation and throughout the duration of the investigation. Various projects are the subject of public inquiry such as planning documents [...].

"Presented in a survey file, the project includes graphic documents (plans), various explanatory documents [...] and a survey register designed to receive observations of the public throughout the investigation."[1]

J. de Muer, cofounder Bureau des Guides GR2013:

"Starting from an idea, an identified need, and turning it into a project, a public policy, involving and informing the inhabitants, is the classic scheme of a community. The development of the project usually targets completion as its final goal, with everyone invited to join the process without the opportunity to have a significant influence on the targeted goal, on the common history that this process would create. The rules of the game are rigged, and as a result, there is little final appropriation or even conflict, and in the long run, a general citizens' disinterest in public affairs. To survey the territory and to take the time to assess it, to measure its functions and uses over time, to meet its users and actors without necessarily having a project in sight, is to give oneself the possibility of arriving at a more collective narrative, the foundation of more just achievements."[2]

1   François Coletti et al., *Enquête publique unique relative au plui du territoire Marseille Provence et aux propositions de PDA sur les communes de Marseille, Marignane, Allauch, Septèmes-Les-Vallons*, 2018.

2   J. de Muer, "Walking Marseille," working paper, July 13, 2019.

NOAILLES

A Diverse Area Under Threat of Collapse

South of Belsunce, across La Canebière, the district of Noailles belongs to Marseille's historical center. Offering cheap housing, Noailles became a more popular destination for newcomers and humble populations in the 2000s. Yet after November 5, 2018, the Noailles district would never be the same again. That morning, two houses on Rue d'Aubagne collapsed, killing eight inhabitants and forcing hundreds others to evacuate the neighborhood. The municipality's questionable response—which blamed the tragedy on rain rather than mismanagement—triggered a wave of demonstrations denouncing governmental shortcomings and calling for an end to unsafe housing. Already in 2015, a report had listed more than 40,000 apartments as potentially dangerous, putting some 100,000 people at risk, an assessment followed by little official action.[3] The structures that fell were of the *trois-fenêtres* typology, and the tragic event points to poor maintenance by local landlords. The panicked reaction of the authorities to pronounce many of these buildings uninhabitable (via the process of *arrêté de péril*) triggered a large-scale evacuation of residents. No long-term satisfying solution was provided, leaving some inhabitants to stay in hotels for up to a year in a neighborhood where public facilities are scarce and approximately 80 percent of the residents are eligible for social housing.[4] Following the collapse, the 5th of November union manifesto, drafted by local groups, demanded a transparent, inclusive plan rather than top-down profit-driven schemes, and a decent rehousing process.[5]

0   20 m

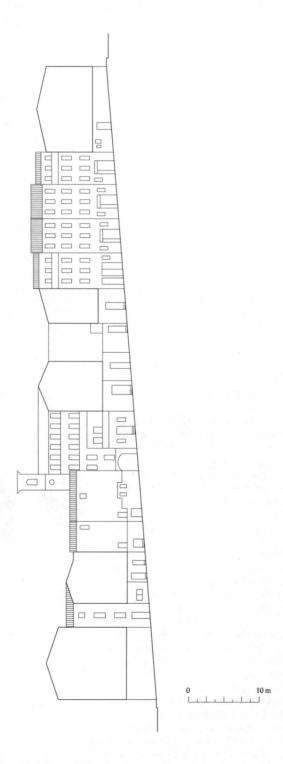

0   10 m

Block typology with inner courtyards

1 Ludovic Bonduel, "Gentrification Policies and Urban Protests in Marseille," Urban Media Lab, February 11, 2019, http://labgov .city/theurbanmedialab/gentrification -policies-and-urban-protests-in-marseille/.

2 Angelique Chrisafis, "Marseille Falls Apart: Why Is France's Second City Crumbling?," *Guardian*, March 21, 2019. https://www .theguardian.com/cities/2019/mar/21 /marseille-falls-apart-why-is-frances-second -city-crumbling.

3 Christian Nicol, "En matière d'habitat indigne, l'Etat et la Ville ne font pas leur boulot," interview by Benoît Gilles, *Marsactu*, November 7, 2018, https://marsactu.fr /en-matiere-dhabitat-indigne-letat-et-la-ville-ne -font-pas-leur-boulot/.

4 Karine Bonjour, *Rue d'Aubagne: Récit d'une rupture* (Marseille: Parenthéses, 2019).

5 L'Etat, La Ville de Marseille, Le Collectif du 5 Novembre, Le Conseil citoyen 1/6, Centre ville pour tous, L'Association Marseille en Colère, Emmaüs Pointe Rouge, L'Assemblée des délogés, La Fondation Abbé Pierre, Les Compagnons bâtisseurs Provence, L'AMPIL, Destination Famille, and La Ligue des Droits de l'Homme Marseille, "Charte de relogement des personnes évacuées," Collectif du 5 Novembre, accessed August 15, 2019, https://charte.collectif5novembre.org/.

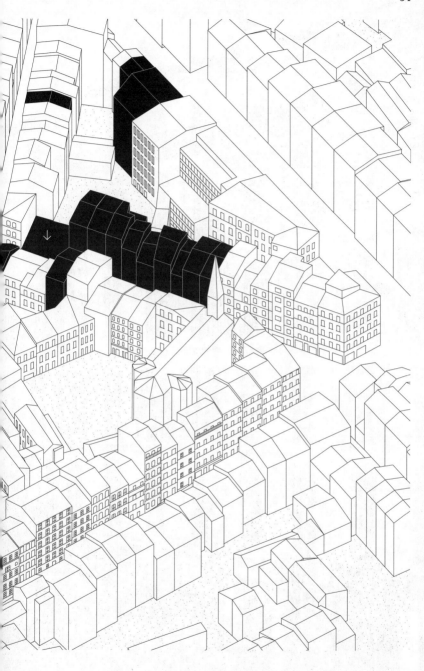

Demolition as policy: After the collapse, the municipality decided to demolish several other buildings. According to the authorities, 23 buildings (those in black) in close proximity to the collapsed structures (white arrow) are at risk.

Domaine Ventre

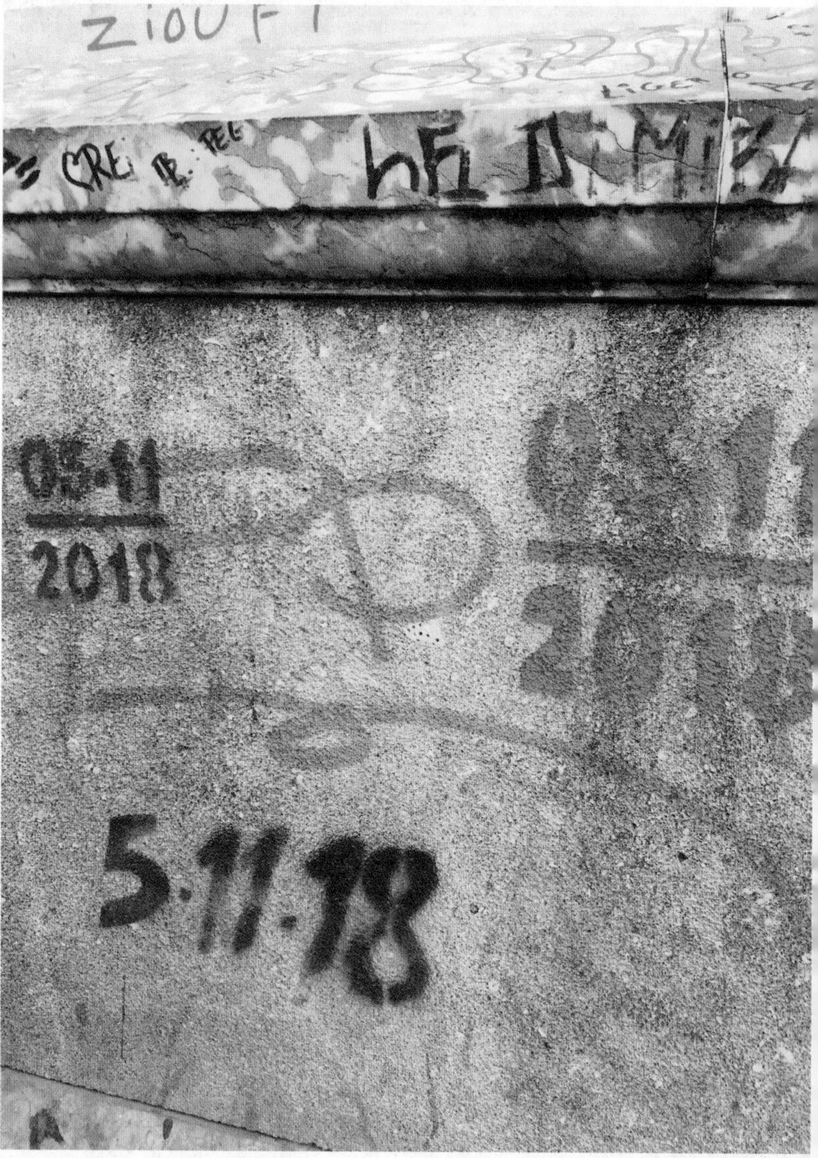
05-11
2018
5·11·18

Ville de Marseille:

"Faced with the tragedy that occurred on Rue d'Aubagne on November 5, the municipality of Marseille mobilized all public services, in synergy with state services, to provide assistance to those affected by this catastrophe. The municipality immediately took care of the families of the victims and also acted as quickly as possible to relocate the people who had to be evacuated within the security perimeter where some buildings could present a danger of collapse. All the municipal and metropolitan means are mobilized, day and night (nearly 350 people mobilized every day), to provide all the necessary help to the people affected by this tragedy." [1]

T. M. Lengellé,
inhabitant of Noailles:

"There is a lack of communication between the actors and a diffused psychosis about buildings collapsing. It makes inhabitants vulnerable to gentrification. The assistance provided appears as a municipal and real estate operation. Technical expertise on building conditions was given very quickly. Owners have been charged with demolition costs with no economic support so far." [2]

1   Ville de Marseille, "Drame Rue d'Aubagne," March 29, 2019.

2   T. M. Lengellé, interview by MAS Urban Design, Marseille, March 19, 2019.

MARSEILLE AT WAR

Paradoxical Landscapes

Nicolas Memain in conversation with
Charlotte Malterre-Barthes and Béatrice Meloni

Marseille is currently in a housing, maintenance, and
governance crisis. Even though you have often defined
yourself as "the only funny urbanist in the world" or
"a gonzo urbanist," you have become a critical voice
among others expressing very serious concerns over
the city's planning and social matters.

> I am a poor citizen and I am proud to be poor. I was
> not born in Marseille, but I settled here in 2001 [...]
> because of the cheap housing market. Around 2010,
> I turned into a walking encyclopedia of the city, as I
> educated myself through reading, archival research,
> walks, discussions, and interviews, motivated by my
> own curiosity for the surrounding environment. As I
> moved through the years from one place to another,
> I witnessed and experienced a constant dwindling
> of housing conditions as rent prices increased. [...]
> Furthermore it became harder to earn a living. What
> was once a good and poetic situation, circa 2000, has
> turned now into a nightmare: bad housing conditions,
> low wages, unemployment.

How did you perceive the renovation of La Plaine (NB:
renovation project of the Place Jean-Jaurès in the first
district that encountered strong public opposition) in
this context?

> The proposal to remodel La Plaine in October 2016
> was in no way urgent for the city. Many more pressing
> issues needed to be solved, and still do. But at the time,

and because Marseille has an enormous culture of failure with most urban projects not getting executed, no one thought that the project would ever materialize.

This is something that can be considered as a form of resistance, or resilience. For example, the Hausmannian project was only partially realized as Rue de la République. However this trend has changed with Euroméditerranée, when a project that was expected to fail did happen.

> Decision-makers say Marseille needs to change. They do not accept the ordinary situation; they want to transform it. But to transform, a city requires something more complex than just the remodeling of a square or a street. The context behind it remains very problematic: housing conditions, school systems, services, and public transportation are completely inadequate. To modify only the appearance of a city is purely cosmetic, simplistic, and populist.
>
> I have observed many renovations, one after another, throughout the years: Belsunce, La Canebière, the Vieux Port. Before being remodeled, these areas were alive and characterized by social mix and a variety of commercial activities accessible to the poorest. After the interventions, former shop tenants and inhabitants were kicked out, and what came instead? Nobody came, nothing happened. Apartments and shops remained empty.
>
> I think that the same story will unfold in La Plaine: public money spent for luxurious flooring and not for structural consolidations. That is what remodeling is: opulent outdoor spaces at street level for shops, while housing conditions remain poor.

How did the population react to this situation, and how is it related to the drama of Rue d'Aubagne?

> History is in the making; we are its witnesses. Let me recount the whole story: In October 2016, the

Société Locale d'Equipement et d'Aménagement de l'aire Métropolitaine (SOLEAM), a public company, announced the renovation of La Plaine and launched a competition. At that time the civic group Assemblée de la Plaine was already very active: they would organize a yearly carnival, public meetings, and a collective sardinade.[1] They reacted to the announcement by organizing several demonstrations. At the time, 2,000 people marched to the office of SOLEAM, opposing the remodeling of the square and calling for a more inclusive attitude by the city developers.

The results of the architecture competition were announced in spring 2017. The winner was Agence aps from Valence in the South of France. Jean-Louis Knidel was in the team together with Paola Viganò, who left the project almost immediately after.[2, 3, 4]

In September 2018, the municipality announced that they would stop the open-air market that took place three times a week in La Plaine's square.[5] Two hundred merchants would be displaced to other places in the city. On October 11, the last market took place. It stopped around noon and, already at 1:00 pm, trucks were arriving, bringing jersey walls to be placed around the square, and the construction began. Residents came and attempted to remove the jersey walls. For the first time in Marseille since May 1968, urban riots and barricades occurred in the center of the city.[6]

October 16 was a big day: ninety trees were cut in the square; every tree was guarded by a police truck with twelve policemen. The demonstrators, far from being expert rioters, were locals both young and old landlords, tenants, unemployed men and women, workers, all together. Massive amounts of tear gas were used against them.[7]

This episode happened shortly before the yellow vests (*les gilets jaunes*) movement started.[8] It created a precedent: citizens understood that the municipality was ready to act violently and that they had to react by organizing demonstrations.

After October 16, the Assemblée de la Plaine organized two big demonstrations: the first was a "sad carnival," with around 3,000 people; the second was the "funeral" of citizens' participation in urban planning (*funérailles de la concertation*). On October 29, a wall of prefabricated elements 2.5 meters high was set around the square. Some tried to demolish it but only succeeded with a few sections.

The wall was repaired at 8:30 in the morning of November 5. They had just finished fixing the first element of the wall at the time the two buildings collapsed in Noailles at 63–65 Rue d'Aubagne. This is an enormously symbolic coincidence; on one side they spent substantial public money for a "fortification" against Marseille's citizens, and 700 meters away two private buildings, part of the city's heritage, are collapsing at the very same moment, killing eight people.[9]

What were the reasons for the buildings' collapse?

They collapsed from lack of maintenance, of course. The building at 63 Rue d'Aubagne was owned by a public entity.[10] Five years before the events, water leaking from the wastewater system was identified. Furthermore, the roof had not been maintained for several years and finally caved in one year before the tragedy.

At that time, because of La Plaine's situation, citizens were already full of anger, sadness, and tears, and not only because of the tear gas. The November 5 collapse was the spark. The legitimacy of the municipality and its governing capacities was no longer recognized. Subsequently, two big demonstrations occurred in November, one to express grief and one to declare anger. Around 15,000 individuals took to the streets and called for the resignation of the mayor (NB: Jean-Claude Gaudin).[11] Both demonstrations were suppressed by violent police interventions.

You mentioned that these were unprecedented
demonstrations in the city. What is the role of local
citizens' groups like Centre ville pour tous (City center
for all) and what are their agendas?

One of the slogans during the demonstrations was
"Qui sème la misère récolte la colère" (Who sows
misery reaps anger). It's quite clear! When the mayor
was elected in 1995, one of his priorities was to stop
social-housing construction programs and assign them
to private developers. He declared that no additional
social housing was to be built, especially not in the city
center. On the contrary, new wealthy citizens were
expected to move in and pay taxes. It was an explicit
decision to kick out the low-income residents from
the inner city. In reaction to this situation, Centre
ville pour tous was founded in 1999 in Le Panier, the
oldest district of Marseille. Centre ville pour tous is
an association that exists to denounce inadequate
public response to social issues; the most urgent
ones being the lack of social and affordable housing
and the inability of private investors to preserve the
existing heritage. Currently, many private owners do
not maintain their buildings, subdivide apartments to
increase unit numbers, and cash in on public subsidies
such as the Aide personnalisée au logement (APL).
The lack of maintenance of the oldest buildings in the
city center (NB: *trois-fenêtres* typology) has been well
known for decades. There were public maintenance
programs since the beginning of the 1970s that have
been transferred to private actors in the past decades.
[...] After the collapse in Rue d'Aubagne, some
technicians alleged that most of the district of Noailles
and several old buildings in the whole of Marseille
needed to be demolished.[12] [...]This is a very serious
threat. We demand technical, geological, and structural
surveys by independent experts. These reports then
need to be publicly shared in order for everyone to get
a clear vision of the situation.

Do you fear that the cycle of demolition/renovation/
gentrification and displacement is what the authorities
have in mind?

> Around 400 apartments have been evacuated after
> November 5 in the central neighborhoods of Noailles
> and Belsunce, based on the *arrêté de péril* procedure.[13]
> Inhabitants were forced to move out; their entrance
> doors were sealed; an eviction notice was attached
> to the door, at times with no sufficient reasons given
> to evacuate the building. Centre ville pour tous, with
> other collectives, such as Collectif du 5 novembre,
> asked for counter-expertise because we really fear this
> situation represents an enormous prospect for private
> developers to demolish the old districts.

Somehow the very material and architectural part of
the city has affected the political conversation. Do you
think that this multilayered crisis is actually able to
affect the political spheres?

> It's like cracks in a painting. But it is not only in
> Marseille. It is wider than that. We lost the local,
> basic skills for building maintenance [...]. Meanwhile
> politicians make declarations that are detached from
> reality, empty words. People know that. Nevertheless
> public funds are spent on ridiculous refurbishments.
> The city is full of scaffolding. Mandatory facade
> renovations are done so quickly that immediately after
> completion, cracks already appear in the plaster. At
> times, the owners have to pay and renovate their facade
> instead of doing urgent structural repairs. We are living
> in paradoxical landscapes: what the city needs is not
> provided, and what is provided is not what the
> city needs.

1 Sardinade is a typical dish made of grilled sardines, but mostly refers to the collective event when people eat the dish together in public spaces.

2 Associate and founder of Agence aps together with Gilles Ottou and Hubert Guichard.

3 Paola Viganò is an architect, urbanist, and professor in urban theory and urban design.

4 Lisa Castelly, "L'architecte Paola Vigano a quitté l'équipe du projet de La Plaine," *Marsactu*, March 10, 2017, https:// marsactu.fr/bref/larchitecte-paola-vigano-a -quitte-lequipe-duprojet-de-la-plaine/.

5 Métropole Aix-Marseille-Provence has been guided by Jean-Claude Gaudin since 1995, the year of his first election as mayor with the party Démocratie Libérale (DL). Since 2002 he is part of the Union pour un mouvement populaire (UMP).

6 To read more about the protest, see Marseille Infos Autonomes, "La bataille de la Plaine," *Marseille Infos Autonomes*, October 30, 2018, https://mars-infos.org /la-bataille-de-la-plaine-3470. See also Benoît Gilles, "Les premiers tronçons du mur de La Plaine arrivent sur la place," *Marsactu*, October 30, 2018, https:// marsactu.fr/les-premiers-troncons-du-mur -de-la-plaine-arrivent-sur-la-place/.

7 Ludovic Bonduel, "Gentrification Policies and Urban Protests in Marseille," in *Labgov. city* (Rome: LUISS, 2019).

8 The *gilets jaunes* movement started in May 2018 to protest the increase of fuel taxes. It rose as an anti-government movement for social justice and takes its name from the yellow fluorescent security vests worn by the protestors. Groups organized protests every Saturday throughout France for several months.

9 To read more about the collapse, see Violette Artaud, "Effondrement de trois immeubles rue d'Aubagne: À qui la faute?," *Marsactu*, November 8, 2018, https:// marsactu.fr/effondrement-de-trois -immeubles-rue-daubagne-a-qui-la-faute/; and Benoît Gilles, "N°63 rue d'Aubagne, symbole de l'inefficacité municipale contre l'habitat indigne." Marsactu, November 6, 2018, https://marsactu.fr /n63-rue-daubagne-symbole-de-linefficacite -municipale-contre-lhabitat-indigne/?fbclid=I wAR0MquwvaRSPbxcegwMue6U-.

10 Le Figaro.fr with AFP, "Marseille veut'un nouveau projet urbanistique' rued'Aubagne," *Le Figaro*, March 1, 2019, https://www.lefigaro.fr /flash-actu/2019/03/01/97001 -20190301FILWWW00323-marseille -veut-un-nouveau-projet-urbanistique-rue-d -aubagne.php.

11 Eight thousand according to the police prefecture. See AFP, "À Marseille, une foule réunie pour la 'marche de la colère,'" *Huffington Post*, November 14, 2018, https://www.huffingtonpost.fr/2018/11/14 /amarseille-une-foule-reunie-pour-la -marchede-la-colere_a_23589554/.

12 See Agence départementale pour l'information sur le logement, "Logement indécent, insalubre ou menacé de péril," Ville de Marseille, accessed July 1, 2020, https://www.marseille.fr/logement -urbanisme/logement/logements -insalubres-et-arr%C3%AAt%C3%A9s -de-p%C3%A9rils; also Tonino Serafini, "Logement: À Marseille, Gaudin balaie l'insalubrité sous le tapis," *Libération*, November 8, 2018, https://www.liberation .fr/france/2018/11/08/logement-a -marseille-gaudin-balaie-l-insalubrite-sous-le -tapis_1690931.

13 Ibid.

FÉLIX PYAT

At the Threshold of Change

Centrally located, Parc Bellevue (also known as Félix Pyat) is both a gateway and frontier to the northern districts. Inaugurated in 1954, it has since accommodated large communities from neighboring countries such as Tunisia, Algeria, Morocco, and, most recently, the Comoro Islands.[1] Parc Bellevue came into the spotlight during the 1990s for being declared the poorest and most insalubrious housing estate in Europe, home to 5,000 people.[2] Since then, the *cité* has been the object of questionable state interventions, including a brutal rehabilitation in the 2000s, when two major sections of the complex were demolished. The objective was to reinsert the estate into the neighborhood, but perhaps also to facilitate police control. Parc Bellevue is located on the edge of the largest urban redevelopment of the city, the seven-billion-euro state-led Euroméditerranée project, but excluded from its benefits, a situation that intensifies the powerlessness of the local inhabitants and migrant groups, deepening the socioeconomic disparities.

---

1   Benoît Hopquin, "La cité Bellevue renaît après dix ans d'abandon," *Le Monde*, January 23, 2008, https://www.lemonde.fr/municipales-cantonales/article/2008/01/23/la-cite-bellevue-renait-apres-dix-ans-d-abandon_1002682_987706.html.
2   Marie d'Hombres and Blandine Scherer, *Au 143 rue Félix Pyat: Parc Bellevue, histoire d'une copropriété à Marseille, 1957–2011* (Aix-en-Provence: REF. 2C éd, 2012).

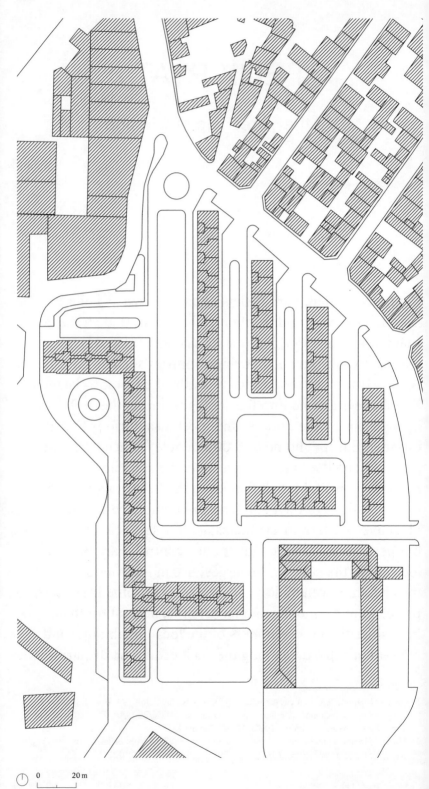

0   20 m

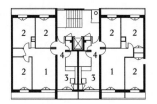

1 Living room
2 Bedroom
3 Kitchen
4 WC bathroom

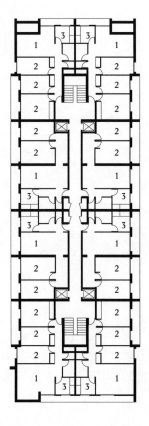

Typical floor plan

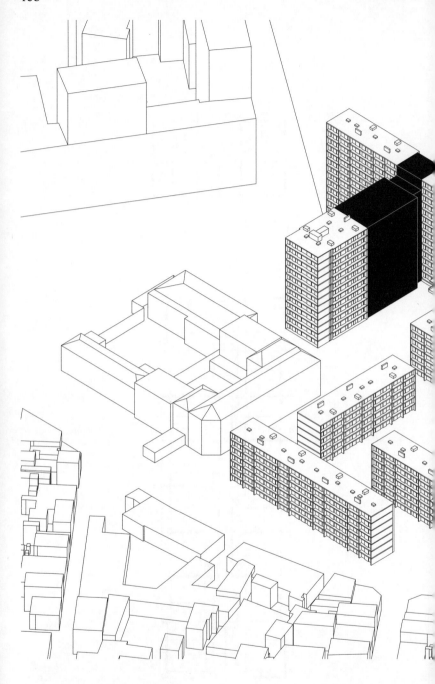

Demolition as policy: Parc Bellevue (a.k.a. Félix Pyat) underwent a severe rehabilitation in the 2000s, with two major building sections demolished (in black). The announced objective was to insert the *cité* back into the neighborhood to solve drug-trade problems. However, the demolitions mainly allowed for better internal circulation and police control.

Parc Bellevue, R. Egger, 1954

PARC KALLISTÉ

Degraded Co-ownership
with Sea View

Built in the 1960s, Parc Kallisté is a large housing complex comprised of nine buildings and 753 units in the north of Marseille, behind the Hôpital Nord. While from the flats one enjoys views over the sea and the city, the estate is remote and poorly connected to the center. Parc Kallisté has seen its population change over the years, from French lower-middle-class Indochina returnees to North African immigrants, Comorians, sub-Saharan migrants, and Middle Eastern refugees. As maintenance costs rose and residents' average income level decreased, the co-ownership building management accumulated massive financial debt and the estate decayed, enticing the drug trade and squatting.[1] Over the years, the state has launched several rescue operations (*plans de sauvegarde*).[2] The latest foresees a central road that cuts through the complex and the demolition of four existing buildings, meagerly compensated by the construction of a few new housing units. In the current context of a shortage of affordable housing, one is left to wonder if reducing the number of available flats is a sensible action. Despite the fragile financial state of both owners and tenants, the complex presents qualities disregarded by the aggressive public-planning approach toward these estates.

1   "Parc Kallisté," Marseille Rénovation Urbaine, accessed August 8, 2019, http://www.marseille
    -renovation-urbaine.fr/kalliste/parc-kalliste-234.
2   Rescue operations were launched in four phases: 2000–2005, issue of first rescue plan;
    2006–8, issue of second rescue plan; 2014, agreement for third rescue plan; 2018, opening
    of Château en santé health center, construction of 1000 m² shared garden. See Marseille
    Rénovation Urbaine, "Ré-urbaniser les copropriétés: Le site de kallisté," Le Forum des Projets
    Urbaines, October 31, 2018, http://www.projetsurbains.eu/re-urbaniser-les-coproprietes-le-site
    -de-kalliste-p491.html.

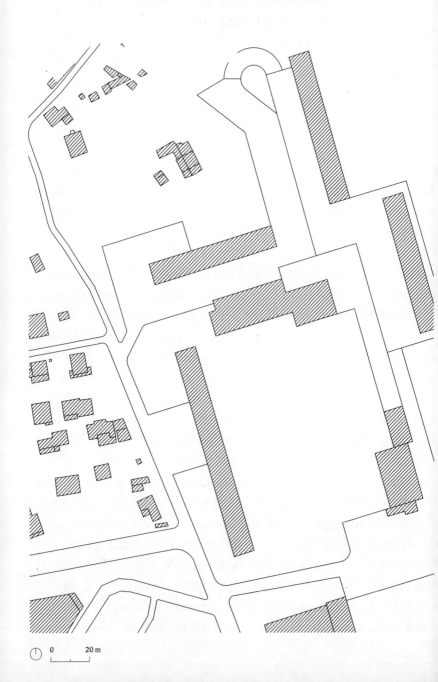

0   20 m

1 Bedroom
2 Living room
3 Kitchen

0   10 m

Typical floor plan

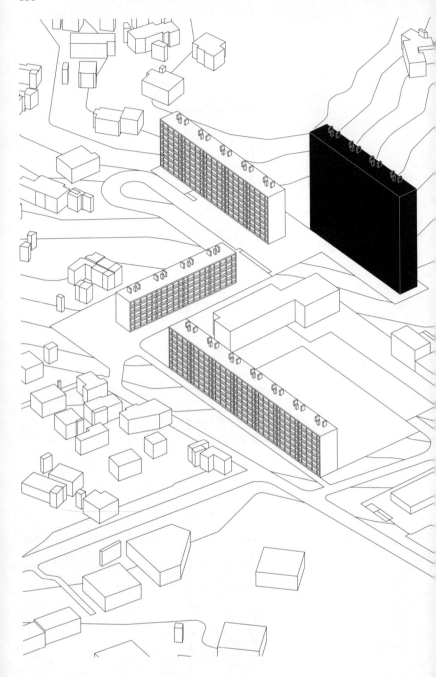

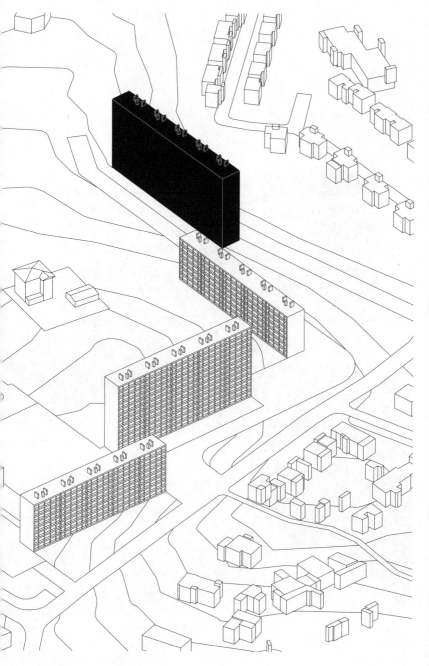

Demolition as policy: The new proposal foresees the demolition of two large structurally sound buildings (in black) and, in the long run, the two schools. A participatory health center occupies the former owner's summer residence, Villa Valcormes. A public road will divide the estate to allow for vehicular through traffic.

Parc Kallisté, A. H. de Vallaurie, 1960s

F. Laggiard, project leader, Marseille Rénovation Urbaine:

"The neighborhood is extremely deteriorated: outdoor spaces are poorly landscaped and poorly maintained. [...] In the large co-ownership of 100 dwellings, the value of the apartments has decreased and the number of owner-residents notably dropped. To remedy this situation, the Municipality of Marseille and the Métropole were requested by the co-ownerships [...] to improve public space, equipment and shops in the neighborhood, on the other hand, with a new rescue plan (*plan de sauvegarde*) to help the co-ownership financially and technically and accompany the owners and tenants of buildings that must be demolished. [...] The goals to be achieved with the participation of ANRU are: restructuring the existing public facilities, creating a new public road, acquiring and demolishing buildings B and H, after relocating their occupants, establishing a health center within Villa Valcormes."[1]

A. Viotti, doctor from Château en santé, Parc Kallisté:

"We try to see the healthcare system as the whole environment: job conditions, unemployment, living conditions, family problems, poverty. [...] When you live in a dilapidated place, of course it has an impact on your health. Problems directly connected to the housing situation are mainly related to the presence of mold and leaking pipes: mainly respiratory problems. [...] People from abroad often arrive with traumatic experiences. They often arrive as single-parent families, with a history of violence. [...] We tried to work on the renovation process with the community. We asked all the kids and the families to visit. They made drawings of the way they imagined the place. We did our best to strengthen the link between the inhabitants and our project."[2]

1   F. Laggiard, "Projet de renouvellement urbain," Marseille Rénovation Urbaine, January 2018, http://www.marseille -renovation-urbaine.fr/uploads/media /LettreProjetKALLISTE_1_jan18.pdf.

2   A. Viotti, interview by MAS Urban Design, Marseille, March 21, 2019.

LA MARSEILLAISE FOR ALL?

Marseille as Banlieue

Marc Angélil and Cary Siress

French people know thy glory
Crowned by Equality, ...
(La Marseillaise, 1792) [1]

Beyond the beaux quartiers of the city proper lies an increasingly
isolated realm cut adrift from the space of law—*hors droit*—and from the
representative framework of a republic that continues to be defended
as the institution of a community of citizens par excellence: the "one
and indivisible" French Republic.[2] Irrespective of this celebrated
constitutional premise born of a bygone revolution, the fractures
inscribed across built and lived space are symptomatic of enduring
distinctions between an "inside" and "outside" of the system. Too
many socio-spatial divisions, in effect, have been essentialized, reduced
to a simplified but effective conflict between good and evil, between
ordered neighborhoods and their disordered obverse on the margins
of society, between the city and its banlieue. In short, the banlieue
commonly represents a form of "otherness" said to threaten the very
integrity of the nation. Although the term *banlieue* denotes first and
foremost a place on the city edge (whether on the periphery or in the
center, the latter being the case in Marseille, which arguably manifests
a banlieue of France), over time it has come to connote that part of
the civic realm that has no part in the body politic per se, except for
its function as a dangerous other. This goes for the people living there
as well, who, according to French philosopher Jacques Rancière,
constitute that "part of society who have no part" and do not quite fit
into the republic's imaginary, save for their portrayal as a dangerous
population.[3]

The stigmatization of a place and people has fanned the fire of anxieties on either side of enculturated divides by consolidating social tensions around what appears to be a problem specific to the banlieue alone. With fears of civil disorder on the rise from already tense social and spatial inequities, not to mention the rampant xenophobia fostered by these imbalances, it is now critically acknowledged that urban policies—be it in Paris, Marseille, or other cities across the land—have failed to deliver on the promise of building a just society. In a country where the Declaration of the Rights of Man and of the Citizen was drafted amid the political and social upheaval of the French Revolution in 1789, political practices since have nevertheless prevailed to compromise the core premise of guaranteed human rights and, by correlation, the even-handed governance of relations between society and space.

Concerning that "part of society that has no part," Rancière inquired whether the violent outbursts against the system that have repeatedly raged throughout the banlieues in the past decades gave a voice to dissent, or whether such instances merely amounted to inarticulate noise that left dissenters unheard as bona fide political actors. In his book *Dis-agreement*, he maintained that effective dissent comes down to who is counted as having a voice, an argument premised on differentiating forms of contestation able to forge a political discourse and those that only resort to violence to contest inequality.[4] Regarding the latter, he claimed that "instead of mobilizing words and acting as if they share a common world with their opponents, the *banlieue* youth resort to violence, and violence in each case gives rise to a wordless scene," which "does not construct a time or a space that can be shared."[5] Still, other scholars disagree with Rancière by asserting that acts of violence do indeed constitute struggles to find a voice in an inegalitarian system but are usually thwarted by being denigrated as mere noise by the public at large.[6]

That said, more successful efforts to mobilize dissent have found a voice with the powers that be, and in so doing have leveraged some sense of hope that marginalized populations might finally find a way out of the "place" assigned to them in society, meaning "there" where they have ended up most likely by default "in the allocation of roles, positions, places, and functions in a social order."[7] The difficult process of breaking with assigned ranks, if achieved at all, entails what Rancière has called "disidentification" or emancipation from imposed identities that make subject types hold—the outcast, the hooligan, the criminal, the addict, the poor, the immigrant, the Muslim, or, in sum, the *banlieusard*, the biased tag for those living in "difficult" neighborhoods.

At issue is whether those with "no part" in a social order can nevertheless become visible and audible on equal terms in the civic realm. Perhaps the most encouraging approach to gaining a foothold in the existing order has come via engaged modes of community empowerment, with neighborhood activists rallying residents to improve their shared life situation by taking stock of existing circumstances and becoming politically active in the process. Measures have included putting local candidates on electoral ballots, organizing stakeholder rallies, participating in public debates with incumbent politicians, coordinating marches to the capital (often originating from Marseille), and compiling lists of grievances that might prompt municipal authorities to initiate overdue reforms as if to revitalize those *cahiers de doléances* so essential as political tools for expressing discontent on the eve of the French Revolution.

To play a part, however, means having a part in the first place. Yet for the multitude in the banlieue that have hitherto been systematically denied a right to represent their concerns, taking part or participating as citizens with a voice is a never-ending struggle, particularly in a society resistant to such actions. Needless to say, common disregard for minority concerns has only intensified amid a rising tide of nationalism and racial intolerance. The push for true democracy is increasingly met with ever more virulent antidemocratic impulses, which Rancière has labeled a "hatred of democracy" aimed at limiting the nation's egalitarian tenets—liberty, equality, fraternity—to a privileged sphere of society.[9] While once forceful enough to have overthrown an unjust regime, the struggle for equity in our time takes place on the margins of a system that remains patently nondemocratic, yet nonetheless prides itself on its hard-won democratic principles.

This intrinsic paradox should make it clear that the problem of the periphery is only the periphery of the problem. Even so, dominant narratives and common sense would have it that the banlieue is the problem. This conviction has warranted the peripheralization of poverty and the impoverishment of the periphery, which in tandem have reinforced lasting prejudices about the banlieue, while masking the urban *problématique* of entrenched segregation altogether. Even worse is that urban policy-making, particularly since the 1970s, has done nothing to discredit prevalent stigmas regarding the banlieue,

insofar as policy after policy have been primarily directed at more effective ways to police those "difficult" neighborhoods and cities such as Marseille, purportedly to the benefit of the sum of society. This leaves little doubt that the divisive order of French cities—not to mention national territory—is one of design, that is, the result of how the nation's skewed means of governing have been translated into material reality: "The way ideas [have been] produced, the issues they address, the materials they select, the givens they consider significant, the phrasing of their connection, the landscape they map, their way of inventing solutions (or aporias), in short their method," as argued by Rancière.[10] Accordingly, the "problem territory" of the banlieue can be understood as the product of a particular method and rationality that has swayed the production of discordant socio-spatial arrangements in varying degrees since the very appearance of the banlieue as the proverbial "place of the ban."

Any prevailing ideology determines how space is organized, partitioned, and occupied. The longer an arrangement holds, the more likely it is to be taken as a justified condition. In the banlieue, the space of the polis remains governed by a policed project of law and order, which is framed politically as the natural order of things. Moreover, political and economic forces work to hold in place, as Rancière suggested, "a common space and its exclusive [and excluded] parts, which makes forms of domination appear as if they are founded on a sensible and obvious system."[11] This arrangement is territorially binding in principle and practice, whereby "society is represented as being divided into functions, into places where these functions are exercised, into groups which are, by virtue of their places, bound for exercising this or that function." By sheer circumstance of being in the banlieue, one is cast as ethnically other, of another faith, potentially dangerous, unemployed, and no doubt poor; and these attributes, so it follows, belong to the banlieue. As long as this common mindset reigns, and as long as those in the banlieue are seen as a threat to the nation, out of place, as it were, it seems all too likely that the republic will remain a divided one.

The issue remains as to whether the disenfranchised of France can secure a voice in the republican order and, just as important, whether that voice will be heard and its demands heeded. Until then, the banlieues will keep revolting, which, in view of the recent past, will only serve to keep a police order in place at whatever cost. To many this will seem reasonable, even necessary, for from the common point of view, burning a car somewhere out on the edge of the city will be seen as nothing more than another case of pointless property damage by apathetic delinquents, a stigma that will no doubt continue to neutralize such outbursts from the outset and keep the core causes out of view. Commonsense perception will just as certainly rally behind the specified state of affairs and thus deny those venting their anger any share in the political community, let alone any say in altering their situation. Predictably, more cars will burn in so many self-defeating acts, which in the end will only reproduce identities already assigned. In this way, the banlieues will endure in their disrepute as *the* revolting milieu par excellence. Then again, to amend the republic's divisive order would no doubt require a profound reflection on the operative set of values that propagate seemingly intractable divides. Such a revaluation might then stir the will needed to dismantle operative identities on interrelated registers—or what Rancière referred to as processes of "disidentification."[12]

(A) Disidentification from within: Rancière qualified "disidentification" as a struggle "to break with one's assigned identity, place, or role in an inegalitarian order" as the requisite move for exercising effective disagreement and gaining political agency to change one's circumstances.[13] Of course, no order—including any identity, place, or role therein—is absolute, for the very possibility of disagreement underscores the fuzziness of being "in" or "out" of place and, by extension, the inherent inconsistencies of a political arrangement meant to keep an order in place. If so, then the mobilization of a community of constructive dissent could, in the best of cases, beget a constituency capable of making a difference in their "ways of being, ways of doing, and ways of saying."[14] The ability to differ in these ways is what Rancière asserted as being political in the most powerful sense of the term—i.e., to become "a part who have a part" rather than remain "those who have no part." Real democracy, from his perspective, "revolves around practices of interrupting and challenging the hierarchically organized social orders by acting upon 'the presupposition of the equality of anyone and everyone.'"[15]

(B) Disidentification from without: While the struggle for self-empowerment involves breaking with an enforced marginal identity, disidentification must likewise take place on the other side of the divide, that is, in common perception, public opinion, the private sector, and the mindset of state officials. Prevailing political identities of this "part with a part" are informed by the republican ideal of

cultural homogeneity that frames any other identity, place, or role
as the other of that ideal. Again, this bears on operative values of
day-to-day practices in the republic that define its order of things. For
there to be any hope for liberty, equality, and fraternity for all, the
root values themselves must be modified, which, in essence, would
oblige a disidentification with dominant mindsets, concepts, policies,
and practices that prevent these rights from being fully exercised.
Recall that already in the late 1960s, Henri Lefebvre had argued for
augmenting the nation's Declaration of Human Rights with an equally
comprehensive declaration specifying rights to the city.[16] His demand
was clear: instead of leaving it to ruthless political power from above
and arbitrary economic machinations, the city had to be managed
collectively as a common good. Furthermore, since "city" for him
did not only mean "center," its "edges" had to be equally addressed
as integral parts of a larger system. Lefebvre essentially called for
the revaluation of constitutional rights, a systemic retooling enabled
by disidentifying with deep-seated biases and phobias at the heart of
the nation's value system. He further suggested that should such a
revaluation ever take place, only then will marginalized areas gain
enough agency to represent themselves as equal actors in the political
community. These propositions were as relevant then as they are today
in their assertion that rights to the city cannot solely emanate from
the center but at the same time must arise from the margins, from the
"mille périphéries" which still figure as the "outside" of the republic.[17]

(C) Disidentification together: A revaluation of the republic's value
system would require disidentification on both sides of the socio-spatial
divide—by those with political representation and by those who remain
unrepresented. Only then could a genuinely inclusive social contract be
redrafted that exalts the right to live in an integrated and functioning
habitat as its core principle. Such a reformed social contract might
lend more weight to calls for "the right to the city," which all along
included social, spatial, and ideological dimensions in the demands
for the right to live, the right to habitat, and, just as crucial, the right
to differ.[18] Come what may, but for revisions of this magnitude to ever
occur and for the republic to be truly indivisible as it still claims to
be, it would have to be refounded on a Declaration of Human Rights,
of Citizenry, of Space, and of Difference, amounting to a *rénovation
constitutionnelle*. Whereas lived space, built space, and conceived space
are all value-informed constructions, they can, in principle, be undone
and reformed in accordance with an equitable value system, just as they

have been undone and reformed under other pretenses in the history of France and its multifaceted revolutions. In that republic yet to come, citizens would have the right to the means of survival, the right to a cohesive socio-spatial habitat as a vital common resource, and the right to differ in how they shape it, the latter signaling the freedom to disagree and resist political, economic, and social discrimination of any form. *That* community might then have the right to claim itself as "the one and indivisible republic."

For a more elaborate treatment of the banlieues of France, see Marc Angélil and Cary Siress, "Paris-phérie: The Revolting Banlieues," in *Mirroring Effects: Tales of Territory* (Berlin: Ruby Press, 2019), 605–705.

1   Omitted verse from the original version of La Marseillaise (1792) when it was adopted as the national anthem by the French National Convention in 1795. Originally entitled "Chant de guerre pour l'Armée du Rhin" (War Song for the Rhine Army), the anthem acquired its name after being sung by revolutionaries from Marseille marching to the capital during the French Revolution.

2   The first article of the French Constitution of 1793, stating "La République Française est une et indivisible" (The French Republic is one and indivisible), has its roots in the republican rallying call "Unité, indivisibilité de la République" (Unity, indivisibility of the Republic) from 1792.

3   Jacques Rancière, *Dis-agreement: Politics and Philosophy*, trans. Julie Rose (Minneapolis: University of Minnesota Press, 1999), 11; originally published as *La mésentente: Politique et philosophie* (Paris: Éditions Galilée, 1995).

4   For the distinction between "voice" and "noise" with respect to dissent, see Rancière, *Dis-agreement*, 29. See also Mustafa Dikeç, "Voices into Noises: Revolts as Unarticulated Justice Movements," in *Badlands of the Republic: Space, Politics and Urban Policy* (Malden, MA: Blackwell Publishing, 2007), 152–69.

5   Jacques Rancière, *The Method of Equality: Interviews with Laurent Jeanpierre and Dork Zabunyan*, trans. Julie Rose (Cambridge: Polity Press, 2016), 94.

6   Ayten Gündoğdu, "Disagreeing with Rancière: Speech, Violence, and the Ambiguous Subjects of Politics," *Polity* 49, no. 2 (April 2017): 188–219.

7   Ibid., 193. Gündoğdu makes reference to Rancière's notion of an ordering of bodies in a spatial arrangement that "defines the allocation of ways of doing, ways of being, and ways of saying, and sees that those bodies are assigned by name to a particular place and task"; see Rancière, *Dis-agreement*, 29.

8   Rancière, *Dis-agreement*, 36, 100.

9   See Jacques Rancière, *Hatred of Democracy*, trans. Steve Corcoran (London: Verso, 2006); originally published as *La haine de la démocratie* (Paris: La Fabrique, 2005).

10 Jacques Rancière, "A Few Remarks on the Method of Jacques Rancière," *Parallax* 15, no. 3 (2009): 114.

11 Jacques Rancière, "Xénophobie et politique: Entretien avec Jacques Rancière," in *La xénophobie en banlieue: Effets et expressions*, ed. Florence Haegel, Henri Rey, and Yves Sintomer (Paris: L'Harmattan, 2000), 215. The subsequent quote is taken from the same source.

12 Rancière, *Dis-agreement*, 29. See also Gündoğdu, "Disagreeing with Rancière," 214.

13 Gündoğdu, "Disagreeing with Rancière," 188.

14 Rancière, *Dis-agreement*, 27, 9, 125.

15 Rancière cited in Gündoğdu, "Disagreeing with Rancière," 189; see also Rancière, *Dis-agreement*, 17.

16 Henri Lefebvre, "Right to the City," in *Writings on Cities*, ed. and trans. Eleonore Kofman and Elizabeth Lebas (Oxford: Blackwell Publishers, 1996), 143 and 145;

originally published in abbreviated form as "Le droit à la ville," *L'homme et la société* 6, no. 1 (1967): 29–35; subsequently published in full length as *Le droit à la ville* (Paris: Anthropos, 1968).

17 Moreau, "Banlieuedenanterre, le droit," text to the exhibition entitled *Banlieuedenanterre*, Galerie Villa des Tourelles, Nanterre, March 2, 2006. Moreau writes: "Le droit à la ville ne peut naître qu'en marge, que depuis les marges, de mille périphéries."

18 For the expression "le droit à la différence," see Henri Lefebvre, *Espace et politique: Le droit à la ville II* (Paris: Anthropos, Éditions Economica, 1972), 145.

LA ROUVIÈRE

A Protected, Segregated Mini-city

This large development was designed in the 1960s with the declared intention to host French colonials—Algerians to whom flats where sold in French Algeria. Self-sufficiency was a key element of the design, with a shopping center, post office, kindergarten, elementary school, clinic, and sports and cultural facilities. Today, it is still one of the largest co-ownerships in Europe, with 8,000 inhabitants within thirty hectares of green space and four kilometers of roads on a steep topography overlooking the sea.[1] Distributed in seven large slabs of twenty- and thirty-story towers, the majority of the 2,204 residential units' inhabitants are owner-residents.[2] La Rouvière's morphology is no different than any other *grand ensemble*. Perhaps what distinguishes the estate from the degraded co-ownerships of the northern districts are the fifty caretakers that maintain its grounds and the high property operating expenses. Moreover this well-kept, albeit slightly old-fashioned housing estate is a segregated village, an open-gate gated community where the rejection of foreigners is an unwritten law.[2]

1 Sylvia Zappi, "A Marseille, l'entre-soi d'une cité sans immigrés," *Le Monde*, April 27, 2016, https://www-org.lemonde.fr/societe/article/2016/02/03/a-marseille-l-entre-soi-d-une-cite-sans-immigres_4858481_3224.html.
2 Ibid.

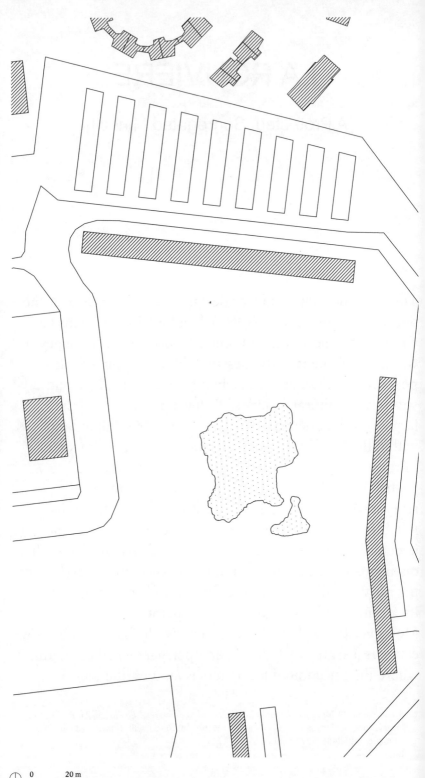

0   20 m

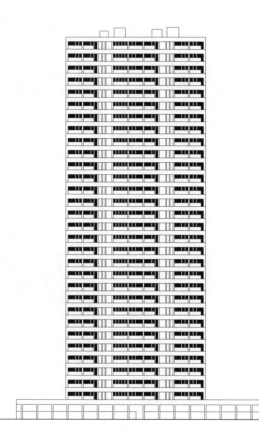

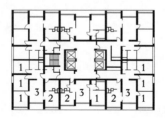

1 Bedroom
2 Living room
3 Kitchen

0   20 m

Typical tower floor plan

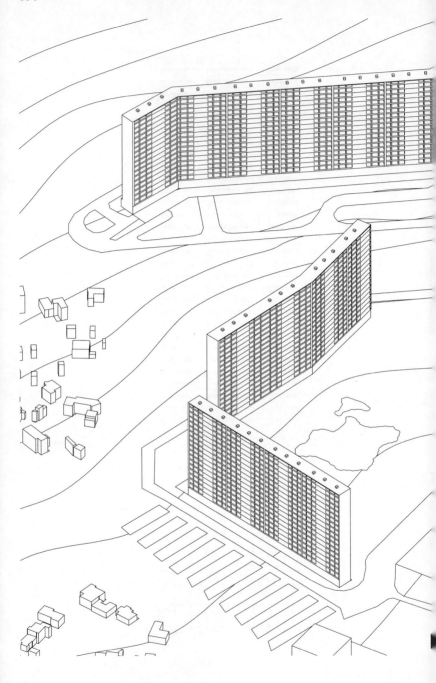

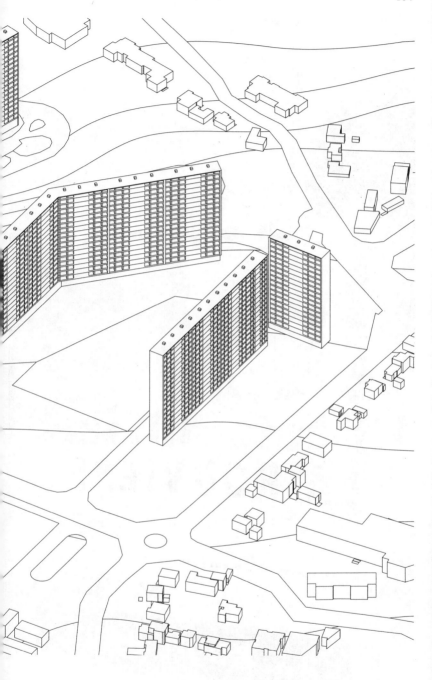

La Rouvière sits atop a mountain range in the southern suburbs of Marseille amid low-rise buildings. No different than any peripheral *grand ensemble*, this rather isolated complex of slabs will become accessible to all only when the tramline planned for 2023 will run. Meanwhile, the complex remains a segregated zone run by a navel-gazing internal management (*syndic*).

La Rouvière, R. Guyot, 1966

POSTE DE FILTRAGE

BUCKLER
06 68 75 00 54

LA ROUVIERE

ETAGE MÉDICAL

83 . BD DU REDON

LA CASTELLANE

Demolition vs. Renovation

Located in the northern districts on the slopes of the fifteenth district of Marseille, La Castellane is a *grand ensemble* originally constructed in the 1960s as part of a larger program of 4,000 units built by semipublic companies. French returnees from Algeria first populated the estate, now home to 7,000 residents originating mostly from Morocco, sub-Saharan Africa, and the Caribbean region.[1] Physically segregated and plagued with unemployment and lack of opportunities, La Castellane is paradoxically well connected to the highway network, which facilitates drug-trafficking there.[2] In response, the state has taken repressive measures and increased police presence while also engaging in costly demolitions to reduce the number of residential units and disrupt illegal activities. However, in the process, residents have been neglected. Even though the estate is materially in good condition, its architectural and urban qualities are given secondary importance, as the state's aggressive interventions focus on surveillance and "pacification."[3]

---

1   Thierry Durousseau, "Marseille XX: 1535–La Castellane," Ministère de la Culture, accessed January 9, 2020, https://www.culture.gouv.fr/Regions/Drac-Provence-Alpes-Cote-d-Azur /Politique-et-actions-culturelles/Architecture-contemporaine-remarquable-en-Paca/Les-etudes /Marseille-ensembles-et-residences-de-la-periode-1955-1975/Ensembles-residences/Selection -des-80-ensembles-et-residences/Notices-monographiques/1535-La-Castellane.
2   Lizzie Dearden, "Gunmen in Marseille 'Shoot at Police' Hours before French Prime Minister Due to Visit," *Independent*, February 9, 2015, https://www.independent.co.uk/news /world/europe/gunmen-in-marseille-shoot-at-police-hours-before-french-prime-minister-due -to-visit-10033468.html; Luc Leroux, "À Marseille, 7 kalachnikovs retrouvées dans la cité de la Castellane après les tirs," *Le Monde*, February 9, 2015, https://www.lemonde.fr/societe /article/2015/02/09/rafales-d-armes-automatiques-a-marseille-lors-de-la-visite-de-manuel -valls_4572697_3224.html.
3   "Pacification"derives from the Latin for "to make peace." However, it is used here not as "the act of appeasing" but to refer to the "pacification" policies of Brazilian favelas by police and brutal actions taken by a government to defeat insurgency.

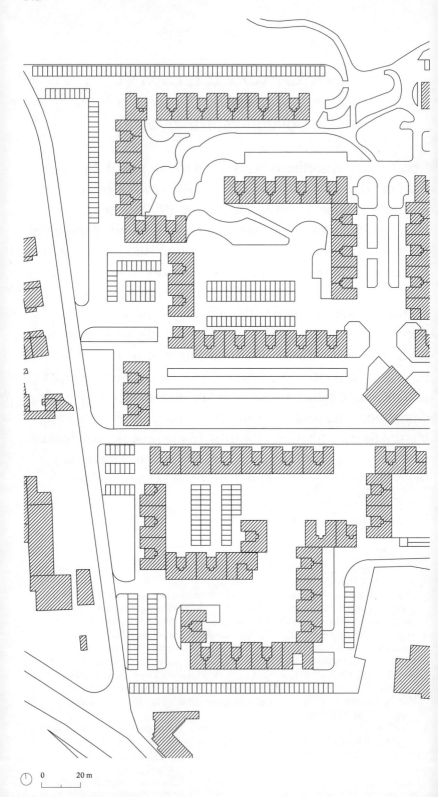

0   20 m

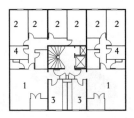

1 Living room
2 Bedroom
3 Kitchen
4 WC bathroom

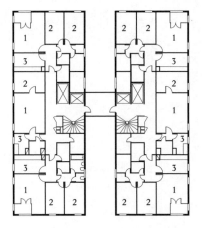

Typical floor plan

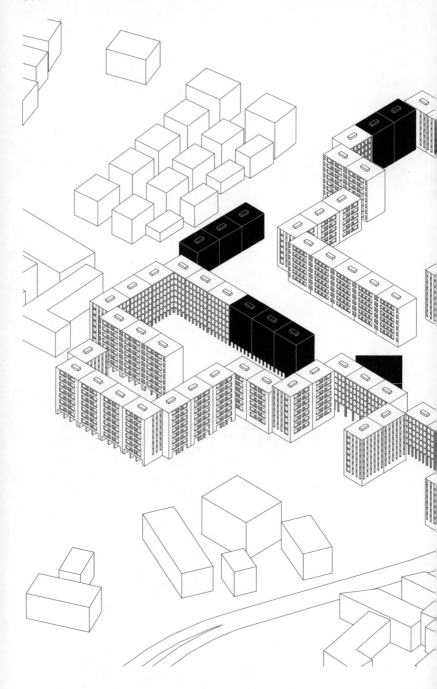

Demolition as policy: Aiming for a de-densification of La Castellane, 200 to 300 units have already been demolished or are about to be (in black), including the former home of famous football player Zinedine Zidane. The planned rehabilitation of some 900 remaining dwellings is intended to enlarge the existing public spaces to allow for crossing the estate—also by police forces.

La Castellane, P. Meillassoux, 1966–1969

EUROMÉDITERRANÉE II

Speculative Urban Planning

Euroméditerranée (Euroméd) is a massive urban renewal scheme initiated in 1995 and located in the northern districts of Marseille, along the industrial harbor. It is a government initiative, *opération d'intérêt national* (OIN), although out of the seven billion euros in investment, five billion are from private sources. The self-proclaimed "Mediterranean eco-friendly district of the future" is proposed to be the new center of Euroméd II, the second phase of the project.[1] Marseille's flea market lies at the heart of the proposed fourteen-hectare development. Old factories and working-class neighborhoods are affected by the project, such as the neighboring villages of Les Crottes and La Cabucelle. These were first inhabited by Italian laborers in the late nineteenth century, followed by a wave of Armenian refugees in the 1920s, and most recently (post-1945), by sub-Saharan African migrants.[2] If successful, the proposed development will displace an existing population of 5,000 impoverished working-class residents to usher in some 30,000 new residents of higher social status, fueling the city's social divide.[3] Urban renewal methods that destroy a historically active industrial district and an arrival neighborhood raise alarming issues about the social exclusion of local inhabitants, newcomers, and refugees.

1   Euroméditerranée, "Fabriquer la ville de demain," Les Fabriques, accessed August 15, 2019, https://lesfabriques.fr/.
2   Florent de Corbier, "Marseille: Le sort des habitants des Crottes supplante la rénovation," *La Marseillaise*, March 26, 2018.
3   Michèle Jolé and William Kornblumm, "The Flea Market of Marseille," *Metropolitiques*, May 17, 2016.

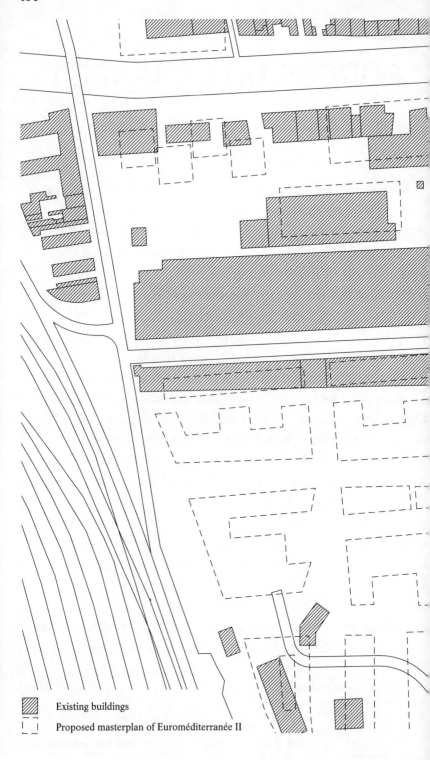

Existing buildings

Proposed masterplan of Euroméditerranée II

0   20 m

Existing urban conditions juxtaposed with Euroméd II's proposal

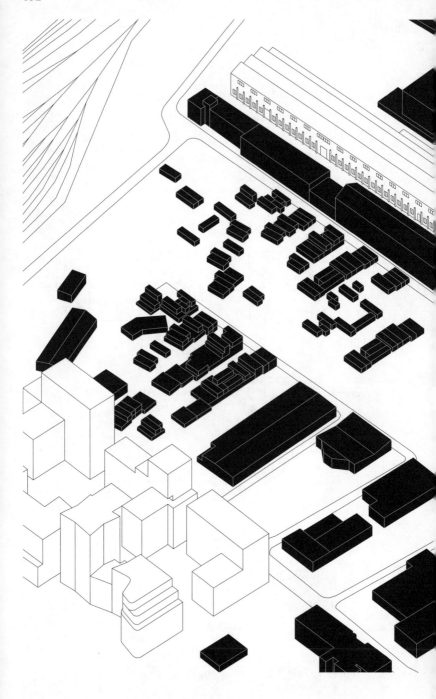

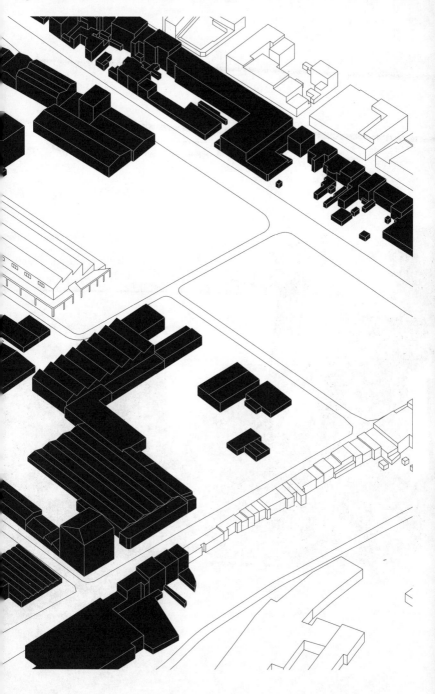

Tabula rasa as policy: The existing industrial and working-class neighborhoods in the so-called XXL plot (Les Fabriques) is to be demolished (in black) and replaced by a new high-end mixed-use block. The market, at the center of the site, will remain as the only trace of the site's original character, though it is unclear for how long.

Marché aux puces (plot of the Îlot XXL)

SANDW...
PIZZA...
PLATS CHAU...
GRILLADES

3 PIZZAS
ANCHOIS OU FROMAGE
11 €

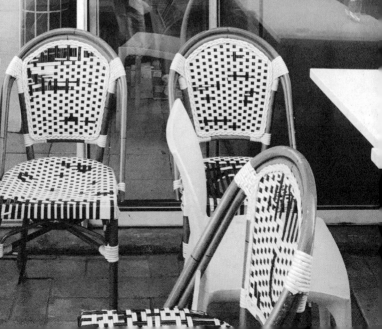

PROJECTS
FOR
MARSEILLE

EIFFAGE

"Here we build a connected neighborhood. Wi-Fi free for all, a tablet per apartment, which will allow one to control their own energy consumption […]. This revolutionary urban concept becomes a link between the north and center of the city. This innovative Allard area will be the pilot of a much larger development across 700,000 m^2 of floor area called 'ZAC litoral' and more generally on the whole extension of Euroméd II, which is an area that will eventually accommodate more than 30,000 inhabitants in the heart of Marseille. […] The people of Marseille must take ownership of this project because it is the city of tomorrow, because it will be connected, because architecturally it is beautiful, because it integrates energy transition, and because it is proud to be the reference in terms of city development. […] Smartseille, an eco-neighborhood of the future, living in the present." [1]

M. Bourrissoux, Arènes

"The renewal operation, named the 'ZAC littoral', must complete its development within five years. The project, promoted by the French government, has set a very ambitious goal. It will host 34,000 inhabitants in 14,000 new apartments. Are the goals and ambitions of the project pragmatic and realistic? What will happen when so many new inhabitants arrive to the project area? They have chosen the area, and established a floor area ratio of 2.5, and they arbitrarily obtained the number of 30,000 new inhabitants. There are challenges to be confronted: it is a floodable zone with a lot of pollution. Moreover it is the site of the marché aux puces, which has a fragile economy. The question is the equilibrium between the market and the existing context, and its connection with the new development characterized by an enormous amount of built square meters." [2]

1   EIFFAGE in Cyril Chauvin, "Eiffage Smartseille Ecoquartier" (Marseille: Eiffage, 2015), 6:17 min.

2   M. Bourrissoux, interview by MAS Urban Design, Marseille, March 20, 2019.

URBAN DESIGN FOR A MORE INCLUSIVE CITY

Belsunce, Noailles, Parc Bellevue, Parc Kallisté, La Castellane, Euroméditerranée II: six projects in Marseille address urban conditions ranging from the dense seventeenth-century central districts to the remote *grands ensembles* and their vast landscapes. Each of these sites tackles a myriad of issues, from shortcomings of municipal responses and housing policies to gentrification risks, maintenance problems, land speculation and predatory real estate deals, social segregation, demolition policies, and architectural failures. Yet these sites also showcase a multitude of solutions, from affordable informal housing to integrative jobs, spatial connectivity, active small businesses, dynamic public spaces, and beautiful landscapes. The unifying entry point to the sites and the proposed projects revolves around migration questions encountered across the city in various and complex forms. The six urban design projects presented here deploy an assortment of strategies that respond to the sites, aiming to make Marseille a more inclusive city.

1. Belsunce 2. Noailles 3. Parc Bellevue (Félix Pyat)
4. Parc Kallisté 5. La Castellane 6. Euroméditerranée II

By disrupting possible foreseeable gentrification mechanisms through smaller plot division and new urban codes ("Density of Ownership," George Papadimas Kampelis, Christina Tzevelekou, Preethi Ashok Kumar); reacting to Rue d'Aubagne's tragedy to save buildings from demolition through urban policy, cooperative housing, and structural retrofitting ("Noailles Calling," Stefania Kontinou-Chimou, Caitanya Patel); devising an economic and spatial program based on building with materials salvaged from demolished structures to empower communities ("Ecology of Deconstruction," Chiara Cirrone, Alexis Schulman); combatting investors' immediate modus operandi via long-term planning ("Port of Entry," Andrea Gonzalez Palos, Beatrice Meloni, Jassim F. Alnashmi); importing a central urban form and its economy to the cités ("Le Cours," Pablo Levine Mardones, Wenjie Shen); or reinventing a controversial urban form by surrounding it with smaller ones ("Petits et Grands, Ensemble," Fai Leelasiriwong, Alexandra Zachariadi), the sum of these projects shows that urban design can lead to a more just and socially inclusive urban environment.

0   50 m

In lieu of the planned project, the large plot at Porte d'Aix is handed
over to a myriad of small private owners.

DENSITY OF OWNERSHIP

Small Plots for a Diverse Urban Fabric

While Marseille is said to have an acclaimed mix of cultures, it is also a metropolis facing a stark class divide between rich and poor. The state's official answer to such problems is Euroméditerranée (Euroméd), the urban renewal project launched in 1995, branded as a hub for commerce and tourism. Despite operating under the status of *intérêt national*, Euroméd is profit-driven, favoring big developers and star architects producing large monofunctional structures. Losing the diverse, fine-grain urban fabric, and marginalizing lower- and middle-income inhabitants along the way, the project ultimately produces social and spatial segregation.

To counteract these trends, "Density of Ownership" proposes a critique of Euroméd at the site of Porte d'Aix by offering an alternative and inclusive master plan to reform ownership modes and access to property. Driven by a few key public buildings, the project plans a diversely sized and priced set of plots allowing for a multitude of small investors. The suggested model of diverse ownership is a contemporary interpretation of past development patterns exemplifying how neighborhoods can be planned and built in a more inclusive manner.

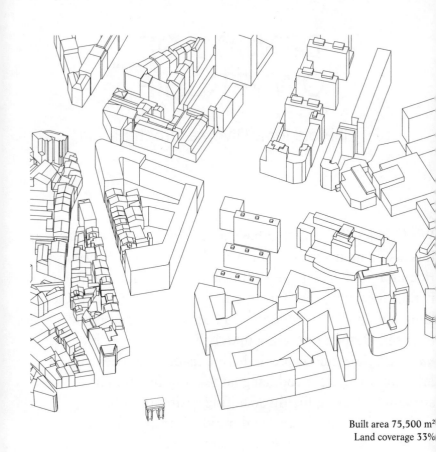

Built area 75,500 m²
Land coverage 33%

Euroméditerranée proposal

Built area 95,500–152,500 m²
Land coverage 47%

Density of ownership proposal

Special Zone Regulations*

Ownership

- Owner can be a physical person, an
  association, or a co-operative.
- Owner cannot be a fund or a company.
- No more than two ownerships per owner.
- All sites should be built within two to four
  years of acquisition.

Building Size

- All buildings should be built on the front
  boundary of the site.
- Maximum BCR (building coverage ratio):
  70%. (I)
- Minimum building height: 13 m (three or
  four floors).
- Maximum building height: 23 m—seven or
  eight floors under certain conditions.
- Balconies can offset 1.4 m outward from
  the main building volume.
- Building volume has to recess 2 m to get
  higher than 16 m. (II)

- Corner plots can be up to 100% BCR and
  have at least 20 m.
- Buildings with a green roof (60% green)
  can extend 1 m higher.
- Buildings with a sloped roof can extend
  2 m higher. (III)

Uses

- Mixed-use buildings get a tax reduction.
- Owners are allowed to turn part of the
  dwelling into commercial space.
- To exceed a height of 16 m, the building
  must contain 10% social housing, and to
  exceed a height of 20 m, the building
  must have 20% social housing. (IV)
- Subsidized plots in cases of social
  housing.
- Temporary uses (vendors, market, events)
  can be hosted in the open public spaces.

* THE ONLY REGULATIONS

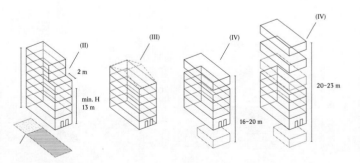

New regulations for individual construction

Group A Prime Location: corner plots facing main squares

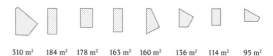

310 m² 184 m² 178 m² 163 m² 160 m² 136 m² 114 m² 95 m²

Group B: plots facing Porte d'Aix

177 m² 163 m²

Group C: corner plots

204 m² 194 m² 169 m² 155 m² 129 m² 112 m² 98 m² 95 m² 89 m² 79 m² 50 m²

Group D: plots facing main streets and inner squares

164 m² 139 m² 130 m² 119 m² 95 m² 89 m² 85 m² 65 m²

Group E: plot-to-plot facing

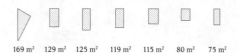

169 m² 129 m² 125 m² 119 m² 115 m² 80 m² 75 m²

Group F: small subsidized plots

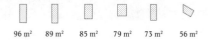

96 m² 89 m² 85 m² 79 m² 73 m² 56 m²

Price Range

High   Lowest Price

Varied sizes and prices of plots

New and renovated buildings allow for common uses of courtyards.

NOAILLES CALLING

Channeling an Existing Legal Model to Empower the Neighborhood

No one can deny that Noailles is a neighborhood in need of renovation. Yet the current maintenance model is dysfunctional, and fails to promote the value of rehabilitation. "Noailles Calling" proposes to deploy an existing legal model; the Associations Syndicales Libres (ASL)—an alternative co-ownership organization—to bring together all co-ownership unions (*syndicats de copropriété*).[1] By pooling the capital of all the unions and thus offering guarantees for loans to banks, the ASL can buy and commonly own property, from a full block to a single apartment. With this money, the ASL operates at all scales, renovates *trois-fenêtres* typologies, reconstructs properties under *arrêté de péril* (the legal procedure that declares buildings unsafe for living), rents apartments to former owners and evicted residents, and revives ground floors and courtyards: in short, the legal model provides a tool to renovate the existing stock without gentrifying Noailles.

1 Les Associations syndicales, "Qu'est-ce qu'une association syndicale de propriétaires?," L'AD Isère Drac Romanche, July 20, 2008, http://www.isere-drac-romanche.fr/?Qu-est-ce -qu-une-association.

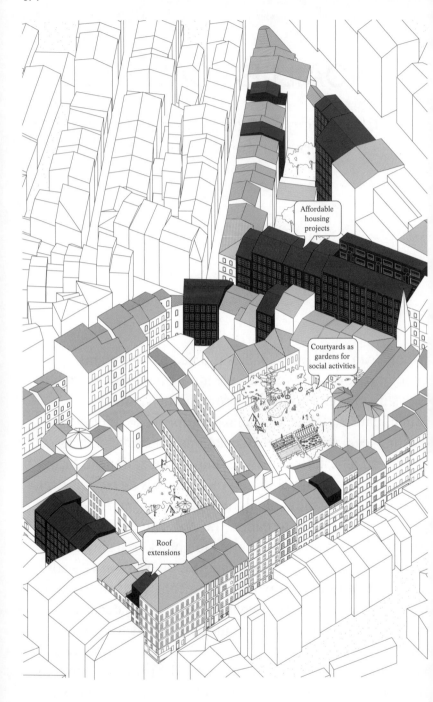

Each ASL works as a community that profits from its properties and promotes different kinds of beneficial interventions.

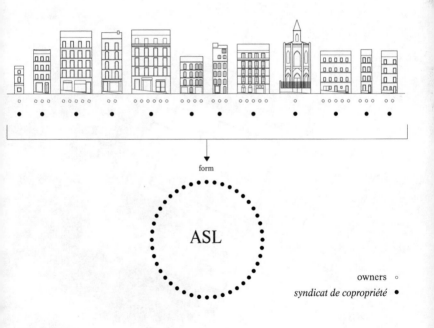

owners ○
syndicat de copropriété ●

Copropriété unions form ASLs to support owner-residents.

The pooled capital of an ASL allows for the buildings of
one block (*îlot*) to be renovated or reconstructed.

A. Family apartment

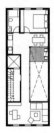

B. Studio apartment

C. Shared apartment

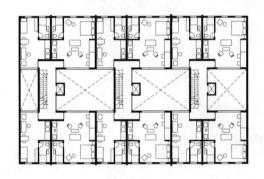

0   5 m

Alterations to the existing stock

Variations of the *trois-fenêtres* model integrate new housing types for the changing needs of users and new types of families.

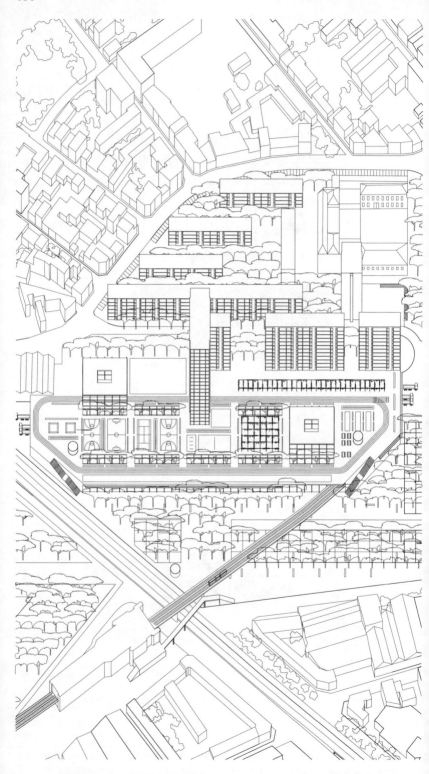

ECOLOGY OF DECONSTRUCTION

A Productive Platform for an Inclusive City

The project "Ecology of Deconstruction" proposes an alternative urban economy to retain and create jobs for low-skilled workers currently ignored by official labor markets and urban development projects in Marseille.

Acknowledging the economic and ecological potential of demolition material, the proposed project aims to use the 300,000 m³ of "waste," that will ultimately be produced by the Euroméditerranée urban development scheme. Capitalizing on this "waste", a socially and environmentally sustainable urban economy will generate new jobs while reducing CO_2 emissions.

Taking advantage of the site's central location and abundance of open space, and answering to a very high unemployment rate of 80 percent, the scheme is a manufacturing platform for the reuse, repair, and upcycling of materials and elements from building deconstruction. It accommodates a public park over the spaces of production and is developed as an industrial co-operative that leases to medium, small, and micro enterprises that are willing to work in this field.

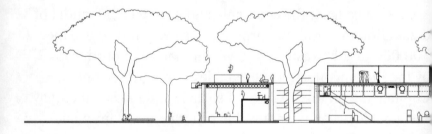

The topography of the site accommodates the productive platform, the sports level, and the public spaces of Félix Pyat.

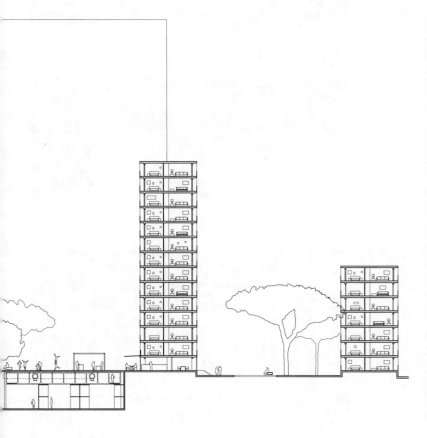

Small ateliers are placed at the border of the productive platform,
ensuring domestic-scale activity in connection with the park.

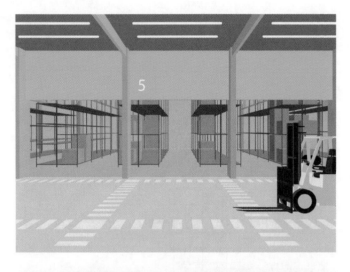

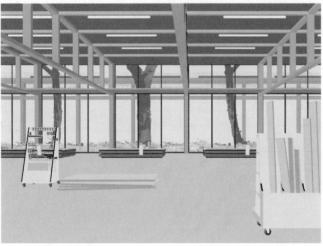

L, M, and S light industries on the platform share functions like storage and logistics of resources and products.

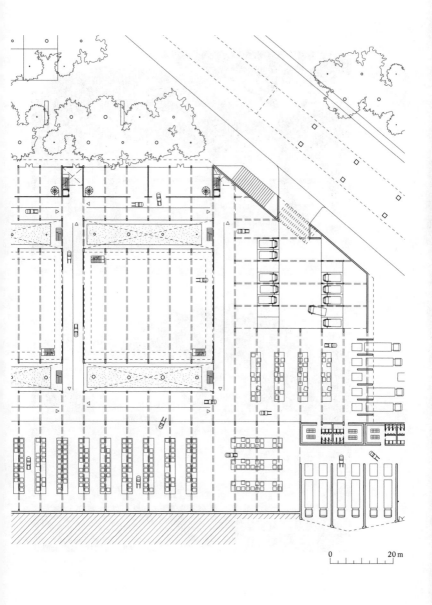

The flexibility of the productive platform allows for the division of
bigger workshops to adapt to the needs of small or medium industries.

The sports level offers a variety of facilities for the regeneration of the Félix Pyat community.

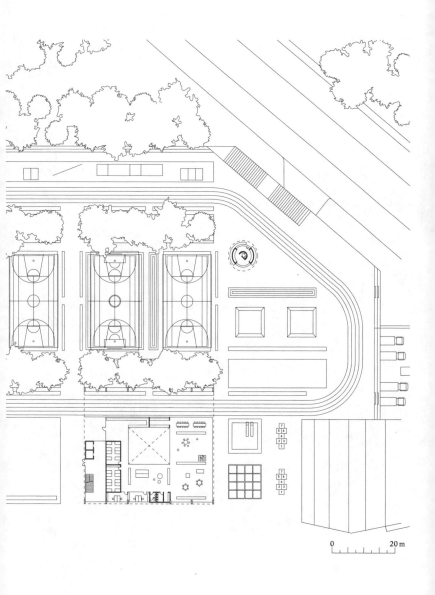

A diverse neighborhood of residential and industrial coexistence

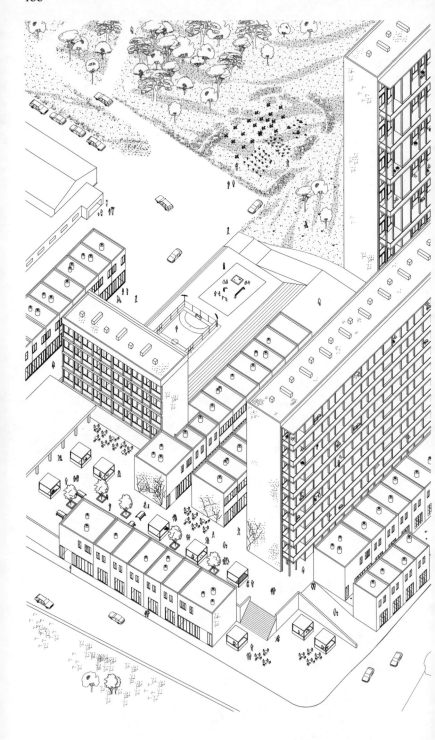

Densification of the ground floor helps to structure
better public space inside the complex.

PETITS ET GRANDS, ENSEMBLE

Small-Scale Densification to Fix the *Grands Ensembles*

Small-scale neighborhoods have proven to be sustainable and successful in creating dynamic urban life, as in Noailles for example. At the same time, some of the *grands ensembles*, such as Parc Kallisté, are characterized by spatial exclusion, social marginalization, and degraded urban spaces, conditions exacerbated by the low number of owner-occupants and high maintenance costs. While the authorities propose a *plan de sauvegarde* for Parc Kallisté, which would see the demolition of four out of nine buildings and lead to a loss of affordable housing stock for the city, this project introduces an alternative rescue-plan model. "Petits et Grands, Ensemble" proposes to densify the estate with small-scale buildings and remodel the existing blocks to optimize their operability. On existing slabs, an additional outdoor walkway serves as a terrace to the apartments and reduces the number of required elevators, thus minimizing maintenance costs. A shopping center modeled on village-style activities is also integrated, and the ground floors of existing buildings become permeable, offering to the neighborhood a truly urban character, with services, offices, and housing.

The low-rise new buildings beside the
existing slabs form a vivid streetscape.

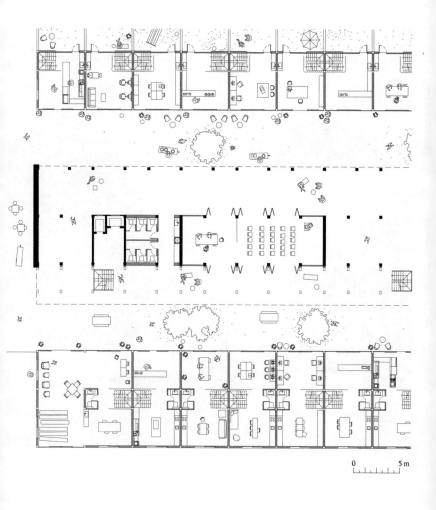

The permeable ground floor of the existing buildings
acts as a connection between the existing and the new.

Small private backyards attached to the low-rise buildings
provide owners with extra garden space.

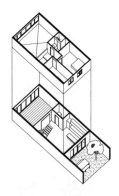

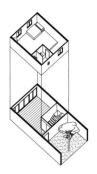

Apartment (56 m²)
Shop-office (20 m²)
Courtyard (20 m²)

Apartment (26 m²)
Shop-office (23 m²)
Courtyard (20 m²)

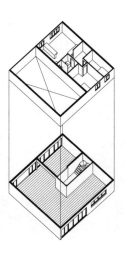

Apartment (30 m²)
Shop-office (20 m²)

Apartment (50 m²)
Shop-office (100 m²)

Four live-work typologies with a variety of living conditions

Small transformations on the back facade of the slabs

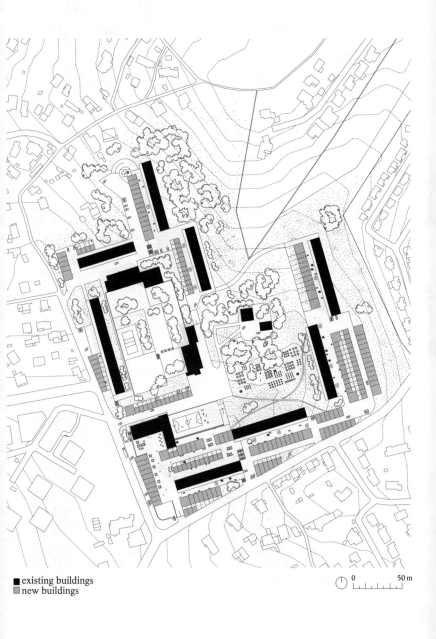

■ existing buildings
▨ new buildings

① 0   50 m

A denser Parc Kallisté with urban qualities brought by
the new buildings among the existing slabs

Cours Julien, Marseille

Cours Belsunce, Marseille

Cours Mirabeau, Aix-en-Provence

Cours Saleya, Nice

Cours Belsunce, 1730 Marseille

Living and working typology.
Cours Belsunce, 1730

"Le Cours": a public-space typology

LE COURS

Toward an Inclusive Urban Form

Inspired by an urban typology common in southern Europe, this project reorganizes the ill-reputed neighborhood of La Castellane as a modern-day *cours* that functions as a mixed-use public space and fosters everyday economic practices. On the one hand, a top-down intervention configures anew the estate's central public space, while on the other hand, bottom-up processes allow locals to shape small-scale transformations throughout the neighborhood in the interior of blocks, where productive and diverse backstage activity sustains the social and commercial life of the *cours*. While the existing central axis is reorganized to establish the "Cours La Castellane," the residential blocks are perforated to create a new network of streets, patios, and courtyards that can be appropriated by the community. The implementation of the Cours La Castellane is based on precise mapping of new and suitable public programs that are directly linked to and activated by the coexisting social and commercial practices negotiated within the more autonomously organized streets and courtyards.

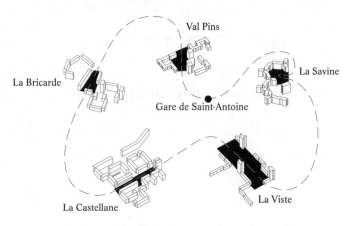

1 A new regional bus will connect the *grands ensembles* to each other and to the local train network.

2 The estate is perforated.
A library and a training center
are constructed.

3 New streets form.
Densification of the courtyard is allowed.
Production spaces, atelier are installed.

4 More buildings are constructed
in the courtyards.
"Le Cours" appears.
The tower is turned into office space.

5 "Le Cours" is shaped as a new urban form.
Surrounding areas start to densify.

Steps toward densification

1. Soft skills and noncognitive school
2. Public library and media center
3. Day-care facility for kids and the elderly
4. Mosque for men, funeral service
5. Mosque for women
6. Vertical common gardens
7. K2 tower converted to offices
8. K1 tower refurbished for housing
9. Commercial strip facing the *cours*
10. Restaurants
11. Office and institutional buildings
12. East bus stop and grocery stores
13. Existing housing typology with commerce
14. Existing typology with a new facade
15. New densification typology 1
16. New densification typology 2
17. New densification typology 3
18. Production units
19. West bus stop and park
20. Existing school
21. Exterior densification

Figure-ground plan

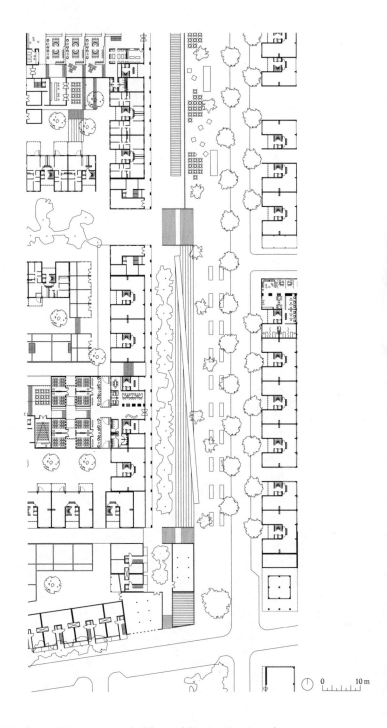

"Le Cours" is surrounded by public, institutional programs
that generate pedestrian traffic.

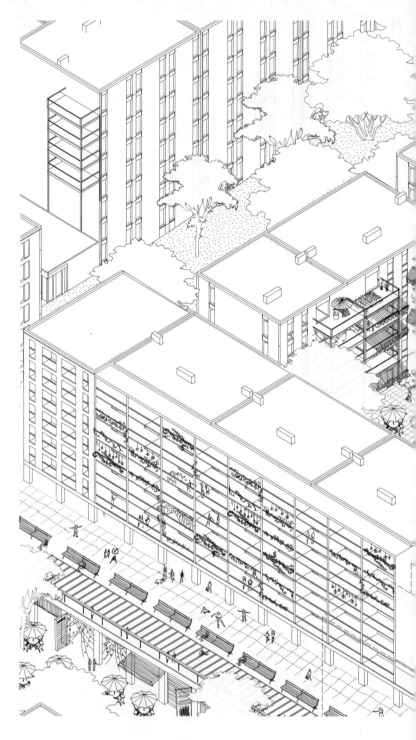

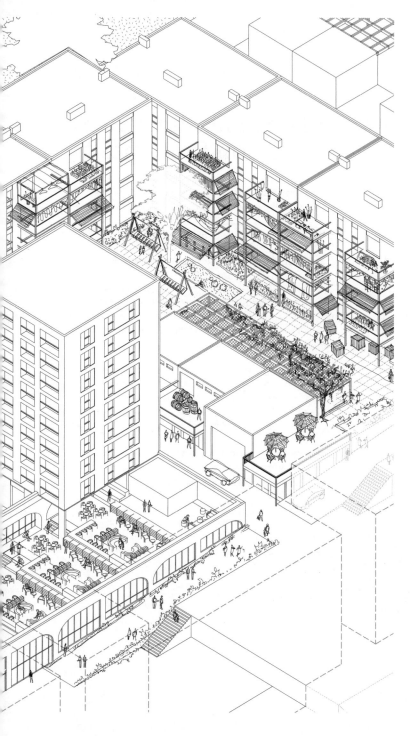

In the courtyards behind the *cours*, activities are less regulated, and low-rise construction is permitted.

Euroméditerranée
Mission Statement

The missions of the Euroméditerranée Public Planning Institution are divided into five branches:

- **Innovation and sustainable development:** to be a territory of innovation and experimentation of urban planning, to test, deploy and promote the innovative services and technologies of the Mediterranean sustainable city.

A misused definition of sustainability neglecting "social justice gender equal and political participation

- **Quality of life:** assistance to the renovation of housing, rehabilitation of substandard housing, production of social housing, improvement of public spaces, creation of sports facilities, development of local services ...

The right to inhabit should supersede the right to property

- **Urban planning:** development of development plans and realization of major urban transformations in terms of infrastructure (roads, tunnels, networks ...), equipment (streetcar, schools, gymnasiums...) and public spaces (squares, green spaces, street layout ...)

Public space is "an extension one's home," especially for migrants

- **Real estate development:** programming and structuring of operations with developers and investors for the construction or rehabilitation of offices, housing, shops, hotels and cultural and leisure facilities.

- **Economic development:** marketing studies, promotion, communication and prospecting to make Marseille attractive, attract businesses, investors or international organizations and create new jobs.

Empowering vulnerable populations through employment is imperative for their access to better living conditions

A critical reading of Euroméd's principles

PORT OF ENTRY

Un quartier pour tout et tous

Opposing the profit-driven instant urbanism of the ongoing Euroméd II master plan, "Port of Entry" proposes an incremental counter-model of city-making, aiming for a better Marseille—inclusive of both current residents and newcomers. Envisioning an urban-renewal scheme that will regulate speculation by targeting different categories of developers, a district for everyone and everything (*un quartier pour tout et tous*) plans a place where diversity of social class, density, and building types will coexist. Resisting the globalized, gentrified renewal projects every contemporary city undergoes, the project preserves existing buildings to accommodate affordable housing, manufacturing and commercial activities, and public space. In fact, the site next to the *marché aux puces* already offers everything that makes Marseille an arrival city: a primary housing shelter for migrants, immediate job opportunities at the market and the port, and cheap food and goods. "Port of Entry" capitalizes on and enhances these excellent existing conditions with new working spaces and affordable housing. The project does not detract developers, but instead phases in the development of the area over time to empower residents and newcomers in order to preserve the place's qualities for people to arrive, settle, and stay.

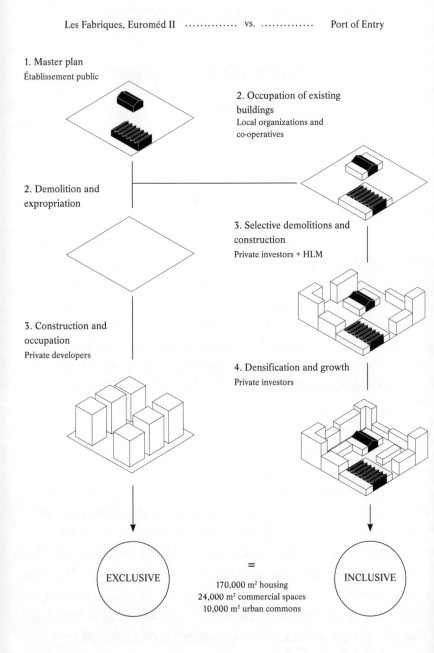

Les Fabriques, Euroméd II ·············· vs. ·············· Port of Entry

1. Master plan
Établissement public

2. Occupation of existing buildings
Local organizations and co-operatives

2. Demolition and expropriation

3. Selective demolitions and construction
Private investors + HLM

3. Construction and occupation
Private developers

4. Densification and growth
Private investors

EXCLUSIVE

=
170,000 m² housing
24,000 m² commercial spaces
10,000 m² urban commons

INCLUSIVE

Euroméd's tabula rasa strategy vs. "Port of Entry,"
a neighborhood that grows through time

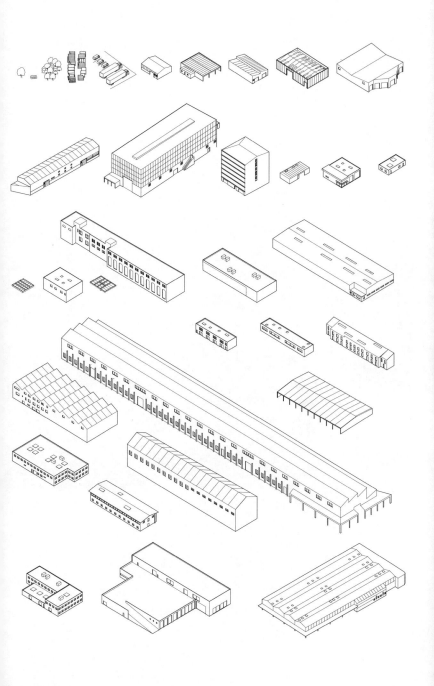

Existing buildings form a real and diverse neighborhood that already responds to the needs of the people working and living there.

A combination of living and working generates bustling streets.

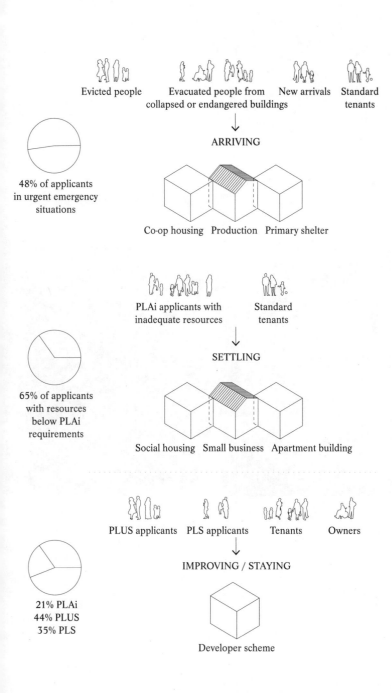

Evicted people

Evacuated people from collapsed or endangered buildings

New arrivals

Standard tenants

ARRIVING

48% of applicants in urgent emergency situations

Co-op housing   Production   Primary shelter

PLAi applicants with inadequate resources

Standard tenants

SETTLING

65% of applicants with resources below PLAi requirements

Social housing   Small business   Apartment building

PLUS applicants   PLS applicants   Tenants   Owners

IMPROVING / STAYING

21% PLAi
44% PLUS
35% PLS

Developer scheme

Steps toward housing accessibility: providing programs to alleviate the housing crisis.

Every courtyard has a specific character creating
a secluded area for the inhabitants.

Different typologies, functions, and public spaces are
intertwined within each block.

PRINCIPLES, TOOLS, AND IDEAS FOR A MORE INCLUSIVE CITY

HOW TO PLAN INCLUSIVITY?

Marseille is paradigmatic of a city confronted with rapid, profit-driven, destructive postindustrial urbanization, a constant influx of migrants from different ethnicities and social groups, predatory economic mechanisms, conflicts between civic and public forces, privatization of services, housing-stock maintenance issues, and state withdrawal from affordable housing production. While civil society has risen to claim rights to the city, there have been few proposed solutions to evictions, demolitions, and the threat of gentrification.

To tackle these challenges and foster a planned urban inclusivity, principles are proposed as codes to design, legal tools reference existing mechanisms that can support social and spatial inclusion; and ideas are compiled in a sort of hands-on manual of prescriptive examples for inclusive qualities. By and large, this section offers an array of perspectives to design cities and neighborhoods that combat social segregation and aim for urban inclusivity.

PRINCIPLES

KNOW THE ACTORS

To develop inclusive strategies and urban tactics, an in-depth understanding of local actors and their social organization is essential. For instance, mapping the existing backgrounds and patterns of the residents before improving a neighborhood provides tools to develop contextual, precise, and accessible environments.

CONSIDER MOBILITY

Mobility is an important factor of inequality. Underprivileged minorities tend to be marginalized at the outskirts of cities. To consider how to enrich the periphery with daily programmatic activities and services is one viable option for more inclusivity.

THINK ABOUT RESOURCES

Urban growth—in the context of neoliberalism—is accompanied by irresponsible resource exploitation. Therefore, to contest neoliberal practices, responsible integration of resources in construction is key, and should be a central concern of the discipline.

INCLUDE DIVERSE FUNCTIONS

To counter homogeneous urban planning and for urban qualities to materialize, a diversity of functions offers possibilities for inclusive forms of living.

ALLOW FOR FLEXIBILITY

Cities are dynamic organisms in constant flux, and spatial strategies need to be flexible and adaptable in order to prove sustainable and include a variety of actors and functions.

DESIGN FOR
SPATIAL JUSTICE

Discrimination on the grounds of sex, race, and social status is spatially materialized in the urban fabric. To plan toward spatial justice is to design for accessibility, affordability, and employment opportunities for all.

REFOCUS ON
AFFORDABLE HOUSING

The housing market inherently excludes groups which are not profitable and abandons impoverished people. Affordable housing should not be given a marginal position in urban strategies, it should be at the center of urban policies to ensure architectural quality. By first addressing the needs of the most vulnerable, it is possible to generate benefits for all.

EMBRACE
TRANSITORY URBANISM

Urban development often benefits private investors rather than addressing contextual needs, leading to eviction, demolition, and gentrification. As opposed to the traditional tabula rasa top-down approach, transitory urbanism is developed at different stages. When private investors come into play, they must be encouraged to coexist with local actors, proving that a new development can achieve the spatial qualities of established neighborhoods.

COMBINE DENSITY
AND DIVERSITY

Dense cities are desirable cities when they are diverse and inclusive. Densification generates opportunities for a better life thanks to proximity to work, public space, and social activities. It can, therefore, reduce segregation and generate social mixing, while reducing emissions and promoting sustainable development.

NEVER DEMOLISH

The urban fabric is by nature subject to aging and decay. Urban-renewal programs usually favor the demolition of the old to make space for the new. However, refurbishment is usually preferable to residents as it is less disruptive. Additionally, preserving existing structures is the first and most obvious step toward sustainability.

LEGAL TOOLS

THE CO-OPERATIVE

A co-operative is a legal autonomous association that is a distinguished form of ownership based on the German system of *Wohnbaugenossenschaften*. According to the Housing Promotion Ordinance (WFV) of November 26, 2003, Article 37, a co-operative is considered a nonprofit organization if it is intended to solely satisfy the need for housing in sustainable financial conditions and not to generate profit. There is no single owner but instead a membership and shared voting rights. The aim is to pool the capital and redistribute it as the members secure their shares by paying a low rent/subscription. The co-operative is responsible for the management and maintenance expenses. Co-operatives are a great tool against high-rents, speculative real estate, and gentrification; they often generate high-quality architecture, as they seek innovative spatial solutions.[1]

1   Dominique Boudet, *New Housing in Zurich: Typologies for a Changing Society* (Zurich: Park Books, 2018).

ASSOCIATIONS SYNDICALES LIBRES

Based on Article 1 of the Ordinance of the 1st of July 2004, related to the syndical associations of owners (co-ownerships), an *association syndicale libre* (ASL) is a legal entity that manages ownership of common areas of several properties, the allocation of maintenance expenses and related funds recovery.[2] It diverges from the co-ownership system as it may own properties such as an entire building, an apartment, or parking lots.[3] If the system is deployed toward the common good, it can become a powerful tool to solve co-ownership problems and undertake large collective interventions. An ASL could, for instance, gradually buy surrounding buildings, refurbish or reconstruct them. It could promote a co-operative effort and be used as a plan of attack for the community's issues.

2   Le Ministre de l'interieur de l'outre-mer et des collectivites territoriales, "Circulaire relative aux associations syndicales de propriétaires," in *INTB0700081C*, ed. Direction générale des collectivités locales (Paris: République Française, 2007).

3   Les Associations syndicales, "Qu'est-ce qu'une association syndicale de propriétaires?," L'AD Isère Drac Romanche, July 20, 2008, http://www.isere-drac-romanche.fr/?Qu-est-ce-qu-une-association.

SERVIÇO SOCIAL DO COMÉRCIO (SOCIAL SERVICE OF COMMERCE)

SESC is another legal tool for inclusivity that could be implemented in the French context. SESC (*serviço social do comércio*, social service of commerce) is a nonprofit establishment operational throughout Brazil that encourages cultural activity and healthy living as its core principles. The economic model of SESC is based on collecting a 1.5 percent tax imposed on private companies corresponding to their workforce amount. SESC members are these employees. They enjoy the entire facilities, while the public can access the premises partially. SESC buildings are typically located in high-density environments where public space is often poor or scarce. Cultural activities such as concerts, dance shows, theater, as well as exhibitions, performances, seminars, and public debates are among the many activities that take place in these buildings, which also have sport facilities (i.e., swimming pools and gyms) and healthcare services (i.e., dental offices). Compensating for the lack of municipal services, SESC's buildings create a sustainable, autonomous, inclusive, and nonprofit space for communities.[4]

4   See Alberto Rodriguez, Carl J. Dahlman, and Jamil Salmi, *Knowledge and Innovation for Competitiveness in Brazil* (Washington, DC: World Bank, 2008).

IDEAS

ANTI-ZONING
FOR HIGHER DIVERSITY
(to provide lively and active public spaces)

The combination of diverse uses is known to generate lively public spaces and activate neighborhoods. Yet planning a compatible sequence of various functions such as logistic centers, housing units, recreational spaces, market halls, and spaces of production has proven to be difficult within the framework of contemporary modernism-inherited zoning codes. A new kind of urban fabric defined through a set of basic urban rules and diverse blocks can form the basis of development. These consist of small, medium, and large plots, while firewalls define their built perimeters to allow for independent construction processes and privacy. Buildings are oriented toward continuous courtyards for light and ventilation, and to increase the level of functional inclusivity each block is developed proportionally by different stakeholders: developers, co-operatives, and individuals.

BUILDING LEASE STRUCTURE
(to build cheaper together)

Housing prices are at an all-time high and therefore inaccessible to a majority of the population. Although interested parties can make use of new and cheaper building systems, the ever-rising land prices create major barriers toward homeownership. The potential of financial structures such as the land-lease model can help to remove speculation on land prices from the equation. By splitting the cost between the end users and the landowner, which separates the ownership of the land and the structure within its premises, the cost of building a home can become more affordable. While homeowners have to pay a fixed rent in order to use the land, they will also lose ownership of whatever was built after a lifelong period. The proposed structure will allow for small investors to collectively access the real estate market.

CAR-FREE GROUND FLOOR
(to promote lively spaces open to the public)

Freeing a ground floor—which is normally occupied by parked vehicles—by consolidating cars vertically allows the street level of a building to be barrier-free, welcoming public access and activity. Including retail shops, cafés, and services such as convenience stores encourages pedestrian traffic in the public realm which, if adorned with seating and trees, can be a popular place to frequent and in which events can take place. Such design initiatives allow architects, developers, and planners to return the space to the city, reactivating public life in the neighborhoods. If a plot is large enough, a car ramp could be added, but one advantage of a car elevator—other than saving space for cars—is that if some of the floors are converted in the future to, for instance, a gallery or gym, the car elevator could still be used for large canvases, heavy sculptures, or gym equipment.

100 financial input
(by municipality or real estate developer)

100 built output
30 financial input for the infill
(by the users)

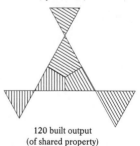

120 built output
(of shared property)

30 financial input   60 financial input
for the structure   for the land
(by municipality or real   (by municipality or real
estate developer)   estate developer)

CO-WORKING COURTYARDS
(to create inclusivity through spaces for interaction)

The public courtyard is a typology traditionally related to leisure and commercial uses. An enclosed space for social gathering is a perfect extension to the contemporary work space, as it facilitates informal interactions and chance encounters. A continuous ground level dissolves the threshold between inside and outside and provides functionality and ease of movement. At the same time, galleries—as integral elements of the courtyard—increase climatic performance with shaded corridors and cross-ventilated rooms. The co-working courtyard is therefore a spatial tool which promotes exchange by alternating spatial qualities: from formal to informal, from closed to open. It creates a plethora of rich spaces where potential interactions can transpire.

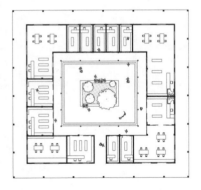

DETACHED PLOTS
(to multiply the freedom of ownership)

Detaching plots refers to turning a plot of land into multistory properties. The transformation of the streets into elevators and corridors, canals to shafts, and street-level plots to elevated plots defines this strategy, which allows for residents to build on individual stacked parcels, making investment affordable for lower- and middle-income people, despite the high land value.

DIFFERENT QUALITIES OF REAL ESTATE IN CLOSE PROXIMITY
(to offer an inclusive range of housing)

A mixture of building types within an urban block has demonstrated the possibility of generating a hierarchy of property values because of differences in view, orientation, density, and access to the street. This strategy, which enables greater social cohesion between different income levels, can be reinforced through an inverse relationship between apartment size and degree of access to adjacent public space. The high-value units in towers at the block perimeter are reduced in size, while cheaper dwellings facing the backyard are enlarged. In this way, the model creates heterogeneity through a mix of different income groups, thus enabling households to select their home according to their priorities.

DIFFERENT USE AT DIFFERENT TIMES
(to increase and densify usage of space)

The lack of free space in our densely built cities has led to a new appreciation for multifunctional surfaces: a seasonal approach to organizing the functions of built surfaces. Using scheduled time frames to monitor usage of space can present a new type of infrastructure for residents and workers in a neighborhood in which various activities, both private and public, can alternate according to their degree of necessity or demand in time. This means that the same space can serve as a car park for businesses in the area during workdays, offer the possibility for workers to play sports in the late afternoon, and function as a screening area or conference space for residents in the evenings and on weekends.

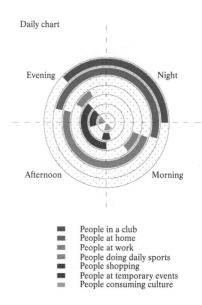

Daily chart

- People in a club
- People at home
- People at work
- People doing daily sports
- People shopping
- People at temporary events
- People consuming culture

DIVERSE PLOT SIZES
(to counter monofunctional neighborhoods)

Plot sizes are closely related to the type of
investors attracted to the site and to the
type of development plans implemented. By
subdividing the land into diverse plot sizes, one
can achieve a wide range of prices, owners,
users, and uses. Without a large profit margin,
big investors will be excluded, leaving room for
smaller investors. The location of every plot
defines the price group to which it belongs.
Each plot can be built according to a set of
regulations that accommodates housing,
public use, or small businesses. An entire area
following such a master plan would blend with
the existing city while fulfilling the dream of
property ownership among lower- and middle-
income populations.

DOUBLE HEIGHT
(to allow for individual interior fittings)

Although many buildings conceptually offer
a broad range of layouts, they are limited in
functionality and growth when it comes to
infill. By increasing the height between the
horizontal elements of the structure to a
double-floor ratio, a larger number of functions
and construction systems can be implemented
within the same building. This increase in the
possibilities of usage offers a hybrid type in
which leisure, work, and living can coexist,
therefore improving the liveliness of the
neighborhood. Even while providing generous
spaces for the development of high-end units,
the double-height structure can accommodate
social housing when subdivided into separate
single-floor units, thus providing different
income groups with the opportunity to live in
close proximity.

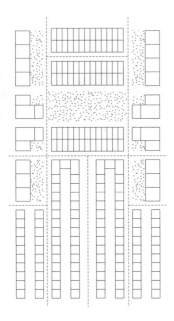

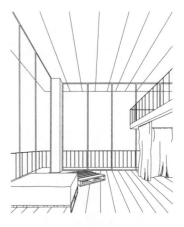

EMBED LOW-RISE BUILDINGS IN EXISTING SLABS
(to provide a vivid streetscape on the ground floor)

Existing slabs typically create an empty and unused public space around them. A tool to create active spaces and make slabs appear more approachable is to combine them with lower buildings. The newly inserted streetscape between the slabs and the new buildings creates a neighborhood feel and gives the illusion that the slabs are of smaller scale. The new ground floor is more permeable and vibrant, and favors social interaction among residents. In that way, both residents of the low buildings and of the slabs will use common public areas, and the commercial center can be developed at a neighborhood level. The aim is to demonstrate that large-scale buildings should never be isolated in residential neighborhoods.

5.5 × 7.5 M GRID
(to create a low-cost functional layout)

A 5.5 × 7.5 m grid is based on optimized dimensions required for three perpendicular parking spaces of 2.5 × 5.5 m plus the width of a parking space's two-directional lane. This grid, when applied on the upper story, allows the creation of a functionally inclusive layout for public, private, and mixed-use buildings. Implemented through a simple prefabricated concrete structure of a slab-on-beam system, it facilitates the construction of a low-cost, flexible, and resilient building type that can host a large spectrum of uses, including parking, work spaces, and residential facilities.

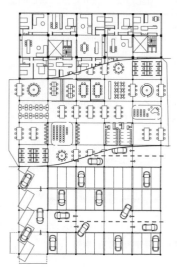

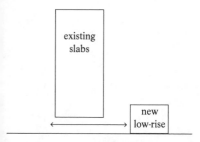

FROM PARKING GARAGE TO HOUSING
(to future-proof the lifespan of buildings)

Lack of parking spaces is a current problem in some cities, forcing vehicles to occupy space on streets that could otherwise accommodate public functions. Buildings must tackle both the housing and parking issues of their site, not simultaneously, but rather sequentially. In the first phase of the building, the majority of the floors are dedicated to vehicular parking. When demand for housing increases and public transportation becomes the dominant mobility mode, the parking spaces are turned into apartments by installing windows on the facade and finishing walls, floors, and ceilings. For this transformation to work, floor-to-ceiling heights must be considered from the start of the project. The cladding should be either removable or placed at every other panel so that the floor is ventilated. When converted to residences or offices, the missing panels are added, creating an insulated floor and providing a comfortable interior space. Flexible and convenient, this system provides affordable housing in dense areas.

FUNCTIONAL BUILDING COMPONENTS
(to achieve larger, more flexible spaces at a lower price)

Industrial building components and standardized construction systems provide economically interesting alternatives to materials used in classical real estate developments. For instance, a production hall can demonstrate how industrial typologies and materials can be repurposed to respond to the current housing needs. The primary structure would be built from standardized pre-cast concrete elements and galvanized steel-frame construction. This construction technique allows for the use of building components like a saw-tooth roof, sandwich panels, pre-cast slabs, columns or beams, and corrugated sheets. These basic building components can create interesting spatial qualities for the dwelling units while offering low-cost construction materials.

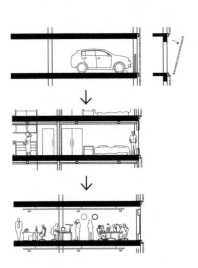

A HINGE BUILDING
(which functions as a portal between different levels of publicness)

When an urban strategy proposes and clearly defines areas with a different public, semi-public, or private domain, at least one hinge building is needed. This is because the hinge building can establish fluid and safe contact between the two types of areas in order to allow for safe passage and foster a mutually beneficial relationship. The programs of the building need to benefit areas such as a community library, a school, or a day-care center. The building could be accessed by both sides through both common and independent spaces.

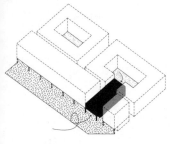

INCLUSIVE RECONSTRUCTION THROUGH COOPERATION
(to combine smaller plots for a large collective scheme)

Small parcels of land in prime locations are often bought out by private developers, which pushes the residents out of their neighborhood. Alternatively, these small plots can be bought by a residents' co-operative formed by small resident-owners and resident-landowners. The financial capital can be constituted by private, associative, and public contributions. The co-operative would unite the desired plot to build a collective infrastructure. As a leading figure, it would offer support for the creation of other co-operatives, renovations underway, and community programs for the residents of the neighborhood. This model would preserve and enrich the social fabric, while protecting it from dubious real estate transactions.

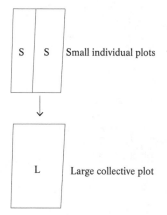

S S Small individual plots

L Large collective plot

INDUSTRIAL HOTEL
(to bring production spaces into
neighborhoods)

SMEs (small and medium-sized enterprises)
are widely responsible for driving innovation
in many economic sectors as well as
providing employment for thousands of
people. The industrial hotel is a typology of
flexible urban factories based on the idea of
supporting industrial growth of SMEs within
neighborhoods where living and working can
happen in close proximity. This concept also
entails flexible allocation of space, allowing for
small leasable units where companies can take
up residence and expand over time. Retaining
industrial spaces is vital for macroeconomic
strategies of resisting and counterbalancing
real estate pressure for residential space
(gentrification), and ultimately for promoting a
dense, productive, and integrated mix of uses
within the city. Clustering uses into industrial
hotels allows for the sharing of costs, services,
knowledge, and expertise of by-products.

INTROVERTED
RESIDENTIAL PLANS
(to enable housing in noisy environments)

The juxtaposition of residential units with
nightlife and businesses in lively neighborhoods
is often the cause of conflict and tension
in our cities. Introverted floor plans offer
viable alternatives for this coexistence: with
perforations in the exposed facades reduced to
a minimum, dwellings are no longer subjected
to outside disturbance. Whereas the role of
the protective layer is reinforced to counter
undesirable stimuli such as noise and air
pollution, the inner courtyards assume the task
of providing light and ventilation to the units.

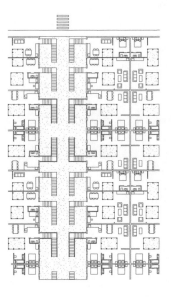

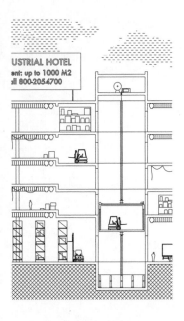

LARGE INDIFFERENT FORM
(to blur differences of its diverse inhabitants)

In order to house all kinds of users, different typologies can be embedded within a larger element or form. Big containers that give an impression of uniformity and consistency can become an appropriate example of inclusivity, as it is impossible to determine the size and individual appearance of a house from the outside. The uniformity and density allow opposite users to coexist because they provide anonymity. In order to maximize the inclusive effect, this carrier of diversity must be considered as a piece of infrastructure that supports the development of other activities and their functioning. Behind its uniform image, there should be housing, commercial and educational programming, and walkable pathways, so that the residents and temporary users can have increased potential to interact.

LESS ELEVATORS, MORE CIRCULATION
(to reduce maintenance and avoid demolition)

Degraded housing estates of high-rise buildings come with low rent costs. Even though they are usually structurally stable, they are very often declared as "in need of demolition" by the responsible public bodies. In lieu of demolition, refurbishment could be carried out with the aim of ensuring affordability for the residents. In order to optimize the use of the structures and minimize the maintenance costs, the number of elevators can be reduced to free up space for the apartments. An exterior metal extension can be added as the main circulation element. This additional structure would also serve as an extra living area for each apartment or new common space.

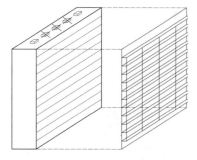

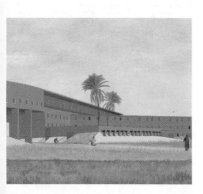

LESS REGULATED POCKETS
(a political negotiation to accommodate the economy of excluded inhabitants)

To allow, negotiate, and delimit zones freed from certain laws requires the goodwill of authorities and commitment on the part of communities. To grant the right of appropriation, security, self-management, the possibility of low-tax trading, and the freedom of self-construction would allow for the reactivation of local, informal economies for those who do not have a place in traditional workplaces due to prejudice, lack of education, or access. The liberated zones could be inside the patios and interior alleyways of the modernist blocks in contrast to the formal, traditional street, thus enriching the diversity of the area.

LOGGIA HOUSE
(to create an adaptable buffer zone)

High construction costs together with a scarcity of space create the need for more adaptable housing typologies. Buildings with a fixed core and a surrounding loggia can provide space for necessary uses and additional area for alternative alterations. This typology can be applied in different sites where the loggia and circulation act as a buffer zone that will be adapted in time. The loggia, when it is more open to the public, promotes inhabitants' interaction and a way to develop powerful relations. On the other hand, it can also have a more private character and serve as additional space for the apartment.

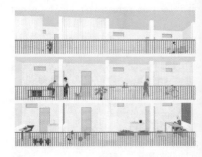

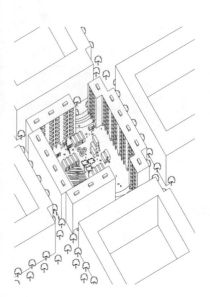

LONG MODERNIST SLAB
(to increase density and social mixity)

The postwar-era *grands ensembles* were intended to solve the housing crisis. These modernist housing blocks often lacked flexibility and variation of unit types. Introducing diverse types aimed at twenty-first-century family structures can bring new life to the tall rectilinear blocks. The ten-meter unit is created by served and service spaces. The rectilinear block spans 240 meters from east to west and has a width of only ten meters, leaving the ground for the city. The canonical orientation provides unimpeded views and allows sun to enter for all residents. The footprint of these new blocks covers minimal ground to allow for farming, landscaping, civic spaces, etc., enhancing the neighborhoods in which they are built.

MERGED AMENITIES
(to reduce costs and protect ownership)

The municipality forces people to sell their properties in a preserved urban context when they are unable to afford the maintenance of the building. Merging amenities could offer solutions: for instance, a new staircase and an additional elevator can provide access to two buildings. Taking advantage of the fact that such voids extend from the ground floor to the ceiling, a new sanitary and ventilation system is inserted, allowing more light to enter the buidling. This idea is realized by establishing relational and collaborative rules between two adjacent buildings, an urban gesture that enables a preserved context to remain affordable.

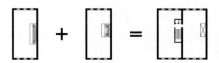

MIXED-USE, AMBIGUOUS BLOCKS
(to provide vigorous and lively urban life)

Responses to housing needs have often
generated ambiguous relations between
vibrant neighborhoods in urban centers and
monofunctional areas at the peripheries of our
cities. As a response to the increasing need
for the return of small-scale retail businesses
to the urban fabric, the image of the block,
a representation of the urban tissue as such,
is used here as a universal tool to generate
heterogeneous uses of the built fabric on
the ground floor as well as to negotiate the
coexistence of large-scale production halls and
residential units within a dense environment.

MOBILITY PYRAMID
(to prioritize pedestrian traffic)

A neighborhood with complex traffic networks
is bound to be segregated not just physically
but also socially. By prioritizing pedestrians,
one can transform existing infrastructures
into a livable street, promoting activities that
would generate investments while attracting
new businesses and services. Thus, by
acknowledging the diversity of traffic agents,
planners can promote the coexistence of
different activities within a neighborhood.

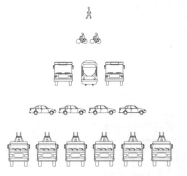

9 × 9 M GRID
(to allow for simultaneous re-forestation and urbanization)

Soil is the ultimate battleground for inclusivity. It is where the concept of infinite progress clashes with the finite character of our world, calling for spatial strategies that allow for the coexistence of human and nonhuman actors. Acknowledging the trajectories that a tree follows during its growth, a spatial strategy with a 9 × 9 m grid suggests a primary act of negotiation as a good measure to accommodate the roots of large tree species. The section of the building can then react to the tree through setbacks. This is where the grid accommodates the progressive growth of the roots and the crowns, as every housing unit receives a terrace under the trees.

NOISE-BARRIER BUILDINGS
(to put different programs in close proximity)

Buildings in our cities often require a protective layer to cancel out interferences between different areas while respecting the viability of various uses regarding noise, circulation, and privacy. When faced with intense noise pollution from the existing programs of the surroundings, a noise barrier defined by double facades, corridors, and services at its periphery can protect a new housing development. Benefiting from these thresholds, the residential environment can orient itself toward the inside of the block and exist in close proximity with its surroundings while being protected from undesirable stimuli.

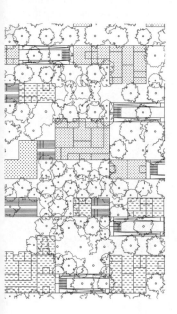

OPPORTUNITY STAIRCASE
(to tackle housing shortages with an architectural device)

State absence in providing affordable housing creates the urge to turn to alternative, self-provided resources. Squatting and self-construction techniques can be used as tools to reclaim land use and rights. An open, shared staircase is added to the existing fabric. The architectural element of the staircase becomes a tool for urban inclusivity, occupying urban voids and reactivating empty buildings. Going vertical makes different levels accessible, provides an infrastructure for resource management and collective uses, and makes existing derelict buildings immediately functional and spatially qualitative. The strategy implies a minimal intervention with a maximum outcome, creating a pilot program in the cityscape that can be applied where needed.

OVERLAYED BIGNESS
(to save space by combining space-intensive functions)

Bringing productive spaces back to the city requires rethinking the means of integration into the urban fabric (spatially and socially). By exposing the productive spaces and proposing a complementary program for the local community, a factory can regenerate a neighborhood and define its identity. A building for productive or industrial purposes needs large volumes, a sturdy structure, big walls, a vast roof, and large parking zones, which in turn allows for complementary activities like sports fields, parks, communal venues, vocational schools, etc. The potential of such symbiotic relationships is a natural integration of light industry into the urban fabric and a density of social activities that fosters harmonious proximity between living and working.

The staircase as access

The staircase as additional space

The staircase as a building

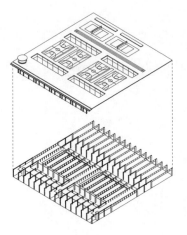

A "PLACE INTERIEURE"
(to extend the possibilities of public space)

The term "public space" tends to be associated with exterior recreational areas. With pre-cast structures and stable elements, low construction costs, and low maintenance needs, a public space can also be in the interior; a public work space, for instance, where structural, electrical, and furnishing elements offer a robust, resilient, and low-cost interior that enables an extended public realm indoors.

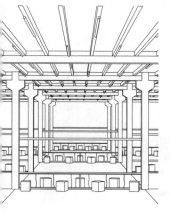

PLUG-IN STUDIO
(to transform a multiroom apartment into affordable studios)

Big apartments might not serve modern lifestyle needs like housing for a single person, single parent, student, or elderly individual. In order to subdivide a multiroom apartment into studios, an additional "tool kit" can be built to provide the extra functions needed, which would otherwise be inconvenient if constructed in the existing structure. For each studio, the tool kit consists of a bathroom and a loggia as a space that the residents can adapt according to their needs. As a result, a higher number of low-cost apartments can be provided.

A PUBLIC-PRIVATE DIPOLE
(to ensure the maintenance of public buildings)

Public buildings often suffer from decay
because of cuts to their maintenance budgets.
Including privately run amenities from the start
to generate revenue from rent in a state-funded
and -owned construction would allow for these
public spaces to gain additional funds for
their management. The proportion of these
supportive "parasites" should be well balanced
in the building, creating a programmatically
inclusive use of the spaces.

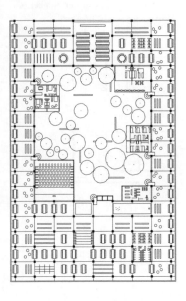

RAISED PATIOS
(to create relations between neighbors)

Courtyards are considered a spatial medium
between inside and outside. When shared,
a courtyard can act as a common ground
between users where meaningful relationships
can be cultivated. Modernist high-rise
buildings—due to the spatial uniformity of their
interiors—often fail to provide solutions to
such diverse users' needs. Shared courtyards
in the form of spacious balconies integrated
into the facade of a high-rise building can have
a beneficial impact on the lives of residents.
They facilitate interaction between neighbors,
positively impact the common life of the
neighborhood, and respond to the scarcity of
space.

RESIDENTIAL MELDED WITH PRODUCTIVE
(to reactivate industrial buildings with complementary functions)

Postindustrial cities tend to relegate brownfield sites to the outskirts, driving out production from the consolidated city. In parallel, factories placed on the city's edge are continuously absorbed in the process of urban expansion while the price of the land is increased. As a consequence, industrial areas are usually dismantled. However, these structures hold job opportunities and social capital. A productive city is one that maintains the existing environment and preserves light industry, combining it with residential and commercial functions. By building new additions to factories, synergistic spatial qualities are created. Workshops, depots, and laboratories can be integrated with new residences to empower new and old inhabitants. The aim of this adaptive method is to reactivate productive functions within the city, all while alleviating the real estate pressures provoked by urban development.

SEASONAL ROOM
(to achieve spacious and flexible apartments)

Contemporary apartments fail to offer programmatically flexible spaces, as each room is usually designed and intended for a specific use. The seasonal room is added as an extension to the existing apartments, without altering their original internal layout. The extension is configured according to the orientation of the facade so as to allow or block sunlight and air flow. Apart from regulating thermal performance, it also redefines adjacent space by providing additional possibilities for occupancy. Without a predefined program, the seasonal room can be used according to the resident's individual needs and lifestyle, which is a luxury often overlooked.

238

SEMIPRIVATE COURTYARDS
(to promote communal life)

Buildings in city centers often have access to
internal courtyards, which tend to be neglected
or privatized spaces. To tap into their potential
qualities, merging them to create large
combined spaces could be considered. Another
approach is to promote the accessibility of
these courtyards, allowing residents of the
block who might not have access to a garden
to rent them. Collective gardening can also
encourage neighbors to participate in outdoor
activities. Courtyards would then become a tool
to strengthen social ties between residents and
place and improve social life and cohesion.

SERVICE FLOOR
(to offer high-end yet affordable amenities for
the building and, ultimately, the neighborhood)

With many municipalities failing to offer basic
services like drinking water and constant
electricity to citizens, the service floor aims
to create a sustainable autonomous space of
interaction that provides these basic services:
social infrastructure for all. Placed in a
building, an infrastructure floor is equipped
with a public kitchen, a laundry room, drinking
water, charger spot, leisure spaces, library,
and digital access. Accessible to inhabitants
and neighbors, it brings together different
activities and services for people from different
backgrounds and age groups, ultimately
creating a community in the neighborhood.

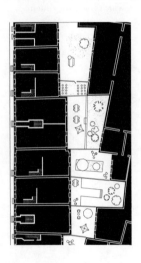

"SEVEN METER WIDE" THREE-WINDOW TYPE
(to allow for more flexible interiors)

A load-bearing facade (i.e., exoskeleton) as structural feature allows for the freedom to articulate the interior layout. Based on the model and size of the building, it permits a multitude of divisions and flexible floor plans, from a luxurious loft to small units, student housing, work spaces, offices, shops, small businesses, workshops, restaurants, internet cafés, clinics, etc. This structural freedom also means inhabitants can change the interior based on their needs while reducing construction time and complexity

SHARED STAIRCASES
(to reduce costs and foster urban density)

As vertical circulation areas require large expenditures in new construction, outlining their efficient use in the planning phase can greatly reduce the price tag of a building. This idea leads to the proposal of an urban fragment that can establish a relational condition between two previously separate built entities. The staircases and elevators are used for their quality as social condensers to form the basis for a sequence of spaces that are designed to allow for a gradient of privacy. The communal spaces of the separate buildings are directly connected to each other through the shared staircase, offering the possibility for both buildings to intertwine their collective environments while respecting the privacy of each dwelling. As a result, this new urban tissue enables a high level of density through the physical proximities of buildings.

Work space Loft apartment

2x (1 bdr apartment) 4x (1 bdr apartment)

A SIMPLE RULE:
ONE COLUMN = ONE TREE
(to avoid urbanization replacing green areas)

A simple line in the building code obliges the investor to plant one tree for each constructed column, allowing for a balanced ratio of building and vegetation. Typologies with large spans between the columns will require less trees, while those with smaller structural grids like houses would generate urban areas planted generously. This would allow for a visually appealing neighborhood with better air quality and cooling effects, while increasing property values (studies show a consistent 5 to 15 percent increase in land prices on tree-lined streets).

6 × 3 M ROOM SIZES
(to allow for adaptability to different functions)

By applying minimum dimensions to programmed spaces within the housing units, it becomes possible to maintain viable living conditions while allocating more space for various other uses. The units are comprised of standardized modules for smaller yet more efficient living and working surfaces. They also include an unprogrammed space that can be used to extend living and/or working areas in order to create collective living rooms for student residences or generous loggias for the different dwellings.

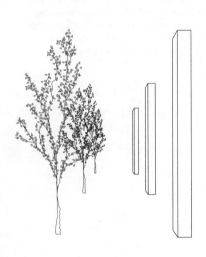

STREET VENDORS
(to define spaces for street commerce)

Street vendors are often affected by the poor infrastructure of our cities; designated parking lots for shop cars help the traders occupy an efficient space in order to sell their products. Sun-shading tents and small tables that are attached to pavement bollards provide a complete parking space for the shop cars. The vivid atmosphere of an open ground floor that functions as a market is completed by the integration of shop cars into the plot. In this way, the street traffic is not obstructed, and the shop cars can occupy the space for a certain time.

THE TECHNICAL COLUMN
(to adapt usage after building completion)

The flexibility of a floor plan is often determined by its structural properties. The distribution of columns on a grid defines the subdivision of the floor plan into minimum rentable areas. Following the form of the column, and the naturally compartmentalized ventilation, electricity, and water systems, access improved and more cost-effective maintenance of the technical facilities increased. Moreover, the inclusion of all technical conduits within the four compartments of a single column enables various building modules to be plugged into the different systems.

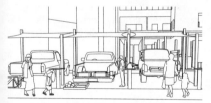

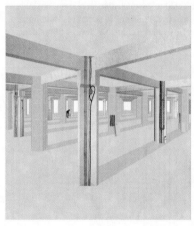

TINY PLOTS
(to make building affordable for families)

Large plots in popular parts of the city are often subjected to speculation from real estate developers to generate an attractive profit when flipped. Narrow plot sizes, on the other hand, balance the scales to favor smaller investors. A hierarchy of plot sizes within an urban block allows for raising the prices of larger and more desirable plots in order to subsidize the acquisition of narrow ones by small investors. Thus, a larger segment of the population has the opportunity to acquire plots and build their own homes. Working with the boundaries of minimum sizes and exploiting the gray zones of urban regulations will counter standardization in dwellings. As housing production will no longer be subjected to cost calculations from a business perspective, housing stock can respond more efficiently to the changing desires of residents.

UP- AND DOWNWARD GROWING BUILDING
(to respond to the changing needs of households)

Built volumes require a certain flexibility with regard to growth and functionality. The townhouse type embraces this incremental approach by extending the vertical circulation above the roof and providing space on the lower floors that can be used for commercial or residential purposes. Residents of individual dwellings can thus rent out the unused lower floors or expand their homes vertically in both directions. Furthermore, by elevating the backyard, a distinction between a residential inner facade and a commercial one that faces the street could be introduced. The additional spaces reserved for parking can therefore be used to extend the multifunctional lower floors of each dwelling horizontally as well.

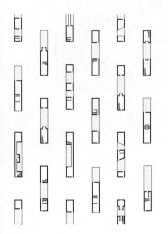

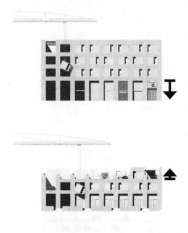

USE IT OR LOSE IT POLICY
(to reduce vacancy)

To combat existing housing shortages, two top-down state policies are proposed to prevent building vacancies, property speculations, and the preservation of natural landscapes within the city. Inspired by the "empty homes" tax in Vancouver, Canada, the first step of the policy would impose a 10-percent tax (market value) on housing units lacking evidence of occupancy for 180 days. The next step of the policy would be confiscation by the municipality of housing units that are unoccupied for a period of twelve months or longer. The confiscated units would then be available for squatting.

"Vacancy Tax" (Empty Homes Tax) Bylaw 11674, Vancouver, Canada.

THE POSSIBILITIES OF AN INCLUSIVE URBANISM

Charlotte Malterre-Barthes and Julian Schubert, Elena Schütz,
Leonard Streich (Something Fantastic)

In its scientific embodiments as well as
in other forms, nature is made, but not
entirely by humans; it is a co-construction
among humans and non-humans.

Donna Haraway [1]

As long as the city has been understood as the manifestation of the
urban condition, urbanism has been the discipline chiefly occupied
with the planning of human agglomerations. However, if we agree with
Neil Brenner's concept of "planetary urbanization," that the earth in
its entirety is about to be urbanized by capitalism, then urbanism too
needs to face this challenge, and in turn must include everything.[2] It
is true that the urban condition is no longer limited to cities. In fact,
every part of land, air, and sea is somehow impacted by human activity.
This anthropogenic transformation of the globe not only affects our
understanding of nature and wilderness but also profoundly changes
the foundations of urbanism as a research, design, teaching, and
planning discipline.

A comprehensive concept of current inclusive urbanism must
include what is considered non-urbanized land as an integral element
in the processes of urbanization. Only then can the economic,
ecological, and social consequences of city building be fully grasped.
By integrating all those functions that were previously subtracted
from city making by mechanisms of exclusion and capitalism, this
new understanding of urbanism aims at the sustainable coexistence

---

1 Donna Haraway, "The Promises of Monsters: A Regenerative Politics for Inappropriate/d
   Others," in *The Haraway Reader*, ed. Donna Haraway (New York: Routledge, 2004), 66.
2 See Neil Brenner and Robert Keil, "From Global Cities to Globalized Urbanization," in
   Critique of Urbanization: Selected Essays (Basel: Birkhäuser Gütersloh, 2017).

of human and nonhumans, of activities, of objects, of forms, etc. Furthermore, an inclusive urbanism shall see the inclusion of material and nonmaterial elements—that is, culture, race, gender, labor, accessibility, religion, resources, ecology, mobility, tenure, construction methods and materials, heritage, vegetation, animals—as equally relevant and interdependent actors for a de-hierarchization of planning concepts and practices, one that challenges current power structures. In a way, inclusive urbanism consistently comprises what has been purged, aiming for spatial justice and a sustainable approach to the built environment in response to the current violent and devastating processes of global urbanization. This rethinking of the discipline of urbanism is central to its positive future impact in response to the highly problematic manner in which current urban development is practiced. From the exploitation of resources (sand, water, and all forms of material extractions) resulting in devastating consequences for both humans and nonhumans, to the generator of universal social and spatial inequalities, planning disciplines are vehicles of environmental destruction in the service of capitalism. This situation is augmented and served by market-oriented land policies, master-planning deregulation, the state disengagement in housing development, and the aggressive capitalization of land, which intensifies environmental destruction and spatial discrimination. The resulting social and economic inequalities, ecological crisis, and enduring violent conflicts propel further movements of people into large cities.

Inclusive urbanism thus encourages all actors involved in the production of the built environment to reassess their role in embracing an inclusive practice and to take into account all social, spatial and ecological factors, while reflecting critically on the complicity of design in the destruction of the planet. Exploring and presenting alternatives to conventional planning methods and concerns, inclusive urbanism is multidimensional in character, integrating a diversity of actors and arguing that urbanism as a discipline holds the key to new visions that embrace heterogeneity. This heterogeneity should be reflected on all levels: in programs and uses, materials and methods, in the promotion of low-cost building, renovation, and adaptive reuse, in tenure mechanisms and ownerships models, financing and maintenance, individual or collective participation, in tactically speculative and nonprofit strategies, lease-hold or interim use. To clarify, a practice of inclusive urbanism would seek affordable building typologies to accommodate multiple social layers, functional flexibility that allows heterogeneous uses and avoids rebound effects; knowledge of all actors that need and produce space; awareness and inclusion of non-human actors; introduction of resources and envisioned policies; design and planning alternatives to existing models of habitation; all geared toward the careful envisioning of a conceivable and promising future.

In the face of the current climate emergency and the dramatic anthropogenic modifications of the earth with the myriad consequences these engender—from migration flows to food patterns—the shift from planning the status quo to one of employing an inclusive urbanism can be seen as both an absolute necessity and the least one can do. In fact, inclusive urbanism should be understood as the starting point from which a deeper, more radical repositioning of the design disciplines can more fully grasp and respond to the urgent and unprecedented challenges we face.

GLOSSARY

Agence aps .... The urban planning agency responsible for the design of the re-qualification project of the Place Jean Jaurès (La Plaine, Marseille), based in Valence, France.

Arrêté de péril .... A procedure initiated by the municipality to force owners of a property to undertake and bear the costs of indispensable works to guarantee the safety of a building when its structural stability is in danger.

Arrival neighborhood .... Drawing from Doug Saunders's *Arrival City: How the Largest Migration in History Is Reshaping Our World*, the term designates an urban district where migrants settle temporarily, where they can find cheap housing and informal work, before moving to other neighborhoods.

Assemblée de la Plaine .. An association of local inhabitants of the area around La Plaine and beyond, independent from parties and institutions, active in contesting the reclassification project of the Place Jean Jaurès (La Plaine).

Banlieue .... A term used to designate a type of residential neighborhood surrounding many French cities that is often marginalized by urban planning policies. It also refers to low-income housing projects predominantly inhabited by modest families and migrant populations, and is used to stigmatize areas characterized by poverty, unemployment, and police violence.

Bidonville .... (*bidon*/barrel + *ville*/city) A slum area or shantytown, mainly self-built, accommodating disadvantaged populations, often migrating from rural areas, at the outskirts of large urban areas.

Cafoutch .... (alt. *cafoutche*) Typical from Marseille and its region, the term designates a small closet, or a tiny enclosed room typically located at the center of the three-window apartment type.

Château en santé .... The neighborhood health center located in Parc Kallisté run by a nonprofit organization.

Centre ville pour tous .... Officially established in 2000, the association fights for citizens' rights to live in the inner city of Marseille, and more generally for quality of life and accessibility to housing in central neighborhoods.

Chanabis .... (alt. *Chibanis*) Meaning "white hair" in Algerian Arabic dialect, the term refers to mostly retired elderly men that arrived in France as migrant workers from Morocco, Algeria, and Tunisia. In Marseille, many stay on a yearly basis in small hotels in Belsunce.

Cité .... The term refers to a specific urban form combining residential units and other services, forming an enclosed complex often built at the periphery of cities.

Cité-jardin .... The garden city is an urban and social concept based on ecology and cooperation, envisioned by Ebenezer Howard in the late nineteenth century. It influenced urban planning and utopias for over a century.

Cité Radieuse .... First an utopia designed by Le Corbusier in the 1920s, the term is now mostly used to refer to the Unité d'Habitation in Marseille.

Collectif du 5 novembre . An association of residents formed after the building collapse on Rue d'Aubagne on November 5, 2018. The association organizes diverse actions to challenge the public authorities in Marseille and demand housing rights and social justice.

Copropriété .... Sometimes translated as co-ownership or condominium, the term refers to a single building or complex whose ownership and management expenses are distributed among several owners. The division is by batch, each comprising a private portion (i.e., a flat) and a share of the common areas (i.e., party walls, roofs, entrance areas, gardens).

Cour/cours .... Originally for leisure horse-carriage practices, a *cours* is an urban typology defined by an avenue serving as a promenade, often lined with trees.

Euroméditerranée .... An ongoing urban renewal project managed by the state, aiming to develop the port area of Marseille. The first phase, also known as Euroméd I, lasted from 1995 to 2015 and extensively transformed the urban landscape.

Euroméd II .... The second phase of the Euroméditerranée project, extending north of the city and reaching the *marché aux puces* area, to be completed in 2030.

Les gilets jaunes .... A social movement that started in May 2018 to protest the increase of fuel taxes in France, it takes its name from the yellow fluorescent security vests that are mandatory in cars.

GR2013 .... GR stands for Grande Randonnée, a network of long-distance hiking footpaths, and GR2013 is a hiking trail launched as a part of the yearlong event Marseille-Provence 2013 European Capital Year of Culture by the Bureau des Guides 13, an association of artist-walkers, local inhabitants, and architects, a group proposing projects and activities with walking as a artistic exploration of the territory.

Grands ensembles .... Collective large-scale housing projects built between 1950 and 1970 in France to accommodate a large number of residents in response to the postwar housing crisis.

Les Fabriques .... One of the main urban renewal projects of Euroméd II, it targets a large area located beside the northern part of the port, including the *marché aux puces*. The public renewal agency (EPA, Etablissement Public d'Aménagement) Euroméditerranée has entered a partnership with Linkcity (Bouygues Development) and UrbanEra (Bouygues Construction) to initiate the implementation of an eco-district.

Linkcity .... Linkcity is the development arm of construction giant Bouygues Development and the new name of Bouygues Construction. Linkcity is involved in the urban renewal project of Euroméd II.

Marché aux puces .... A daily market site installed by the Société Provençale de la Madrague in 1987 in a former industrial area, it offers a large variety of goods, from fresh food to antiques, and boasts a popular Sunday flea market.

Marseille Rénovation .... Urbaine Public partnership formed in 2003 by the state, the Municipality of Marseille, and several organizations, it is responsible for the founding and coordination of various urban renewal projects of housing estates.

opération d'intérêt .... *national* (OIN) An OIN is an urban planning operation for which a exceptional legal regime is applied because it serves the common good. The state retains control of urban planning policy in these areas, granting land use and building permits.

PLAi .... Subsidized by the state, the program is accessible for people with low income to access social housing with a rent of 4–5 euros/m².

La Plaine .... Name used by Marseille's inhabitants to refer to Place Jean Jaurès, a large square that dominates one of the seven hills of Marseille. The remodeling of the square started in 2018 and encountered strong opposition by the local communities.

Plan de sauvegarde .... A plan that aims to preserve areas characterized by architectural heritage. In Marseille several plans were launched for endangered or degraded buildings. These interventions often lead to evictions and demolitions.

PLS .... A partly public loan program accessible to people with relatively higher resources that can afford market prices to access social housing with a rent of 10–11 euros/m².

PLUS .... Partly subsidized by the state, the loan program is accessible for people with resources but in need of affordable solutions below the market price, to access social housing with a rent of 6–9 euros/m².

Politique de la Ville .... Since the 1980s, the French state implemented a series of urban policies based on the involvement of local actors to reduce social inequalities between neighborhoods.

Quartiers Nord .... A term used to designate the Northern districts of Marseille, sometimes shortened to les Quartiers, rather derogatory.

Sardinade .... A typical dish made of grilled sardines, and by extension the social event of eating it together.

SOLEAM .... Following the semipublic company Marseille Aménagement, SOLEAM is a local public company engaged in urban management projects for the large public entity la Métropole Aix-Marseille Provence. It has been criticized for the mismanagement of its properties and for the handling of the La Plaine project and of the Rue d'Aubagne crisis.

Tracoba .... Prefabricated modular construction technique for towers.

ZUS .... An urban area defined by the authorities as a priority target for urban interventions.

ACRONYMS

ANRU	Agence Nationale pour la Rénovation Urbaine
APL	*aide personnalisée au logement*
ASL	*associations syndicales libres*
CAF	*caisse d'allocations familiales*
COS	*coefficient d'occupation du sol*
CUCS	*contrats urbains de cohésion sociale*
EPA	*établissement public d'aménagement*
EU	European Union
GDP	gross domestic product
HBM	*habitations à bon marché*
HLM	*habitation à loyer modéré*
SOLEAM	Société Locale d'Equipement et d'Aménagement de l'aire Métropolitaine
MP2013	Marseille-Provence 2013
MRU	Ministère de la Reconstruction et de l'Urbanisme Provence-Alpes-Côte d'Azur
ORCOD	*opérations de requalification des copropriétés dégradées*
OIN	*opération d'intérêt national*
PLAI	*prêt locatif aidé d'intégration*
PLS	*prêt locatif social*
PLUS	*prêt locatif à usage social*
PNRU	Programme National pour la Rénovation Urbaine
POS	*plan d'occupation des sols*
QPV	*quartier prioritaire de la politique de la ville*
SAINA	Service de Surveillance, Protection, et Assistance des Indigènes Nord-Africains
SCIC	Société Centrale Immobilière de la Caisse des Dépôts
SESC	*serviço social da comércio*
SME	small and medium-sized enterprise
SNCF	Société Nationale des Chemins de fer Français
SONACOTRAL	Société Nationale de Construction de Logements pour les Travailleurs Algériens
SOTC	Service de l'Organisation des Travailleurs Coloniaux
ZFU	*zones franches urbaines*
ZRU	*zones de redynamisation urbaine*
ZUS	*zone urbaine sensible*

BIBLIOGRAPHY

AFP. "À Marseille, Une Foule Réunie Pour La 'Marche De La Colère.'" *Huffington Post* (2018). https://www.huffingtonpost.fr/2018/11/14/a-marseille-une-foule-reunie-pour-la-marche-de-la-colere_a_23589554/.

Agence départementale pour l'information sur le logement. "Logement indécent, insalubre ou menacé de péril." Ville de Marseille. https://www.marseille.fr/logement-urbanisme/logement/logements-insalubres-et-arr%C3%AAt%C3%A9s-de-p%C3%A9rils. Accessed July 1, 2020.

Angélil, Marc, and Cary Siress. "The Paris Banlieue: Peripheries of Inequity." *Journal of International Affairs* 65, no. 2 (2012): 6–16.

Artaud, Violette. "Effondrement de trois immeubles rue d'Aubagne: À qui la faute?," *Marsactu*, November 8, 2018. https://marsactu.fr/effondrement-de-trois-immeubles-rue-daubagne-a-qui-la-faute/.

Berland-Berthon, Agnès. "Les grands ensembles: Des quartiers pas comme les autres." In *Pérennité urbaine, ou la ville par-delà ses métamorphoses*, vol. 2, *Turbulences*, edited by Colette Vallat, 255–68. Paris: L'Harmattan, 2007.

Bertagnini, Elisa. "The French Banlieues between Appropriation and Demolition." *Planum: The Journal of Urbanism* 2, no. 27 (October 2013). http://www.planum.net/download/living-landscapes-conference-bertagnini-section-7.

Bonduel, Ludovic. "Gentrification Policies and Urban Protests in Marseille." *Urban Media Lab*, February 11, 2019. http://labgov.city/theurbanmedialab/gentrification-policies-and-urban-protests-in-marseille/.

Bonillo, Jean-Lucien, René Borruey, Jean Denis Espinas, and Antoine Picon. *Marseille, ville & port*. N.p.: Parenthèses Editions, 1992.

Bonjour, Karine. *Rue d'Aubagne: Récit d'une rupture*. Marseille: Parenthéses, 2019.

Braudel, Fernand, Roselyne de Ayala, Paule Braudel, and Sian Reynolds. *Memory and the Mediterranean*. New York: Vintage Books, 2002.

Brenner, Neil, and Robert Keil. "From Global Cities to Globalized Urbanization." In *Critique of Urbanization: Selected Essays*. Basel: Birkhäuser, 2017.

Brenner, Neil. *Implosions/Explosions: Towards a Study of Planetary Urbanization*. Berlin: Jovis, 2014.

Brenner, Neil. "Neoliberalization." In *Real Estates: Life without Debt*, edited by Fulcrum. London: Bedford Press, 2015.

Castaner, Christophe. "Le dispositif HOPE: Hébergement, orientation, parcours vers l'emploi." Ministère de l'Intèrieur, June 20, 2019. https://www.immigration.interieur.gouv.fr/Info-ressources/Actualites/Communiques/Le-dispositif-HOPE-hebergement-orientation-parcours-vers-l-emploi.

Castelly, Lisa. "L'architecte Paola Vigano a quitté l'équipe du projet de la Plaine." *Marsactu*, March 10, 2017. https://marsactu.fr/bref/larchitecte-paola-vigano-a-quitte-lequipe-du-projet-de-la-plaine/.

Chauvin, Cyril. "Smartseille." MP4 video, 6:17 min. *Eiffage*, 2015. http://www.smartseille.fr/film.php?fbclid=IwAR2DtE-liJngta4YV3Qch3b0LxyrECkOg87o7LY7aZuRPcmgiisoxe0Ht0o. Accessed August 7, 2019.

Chrisafis, Angelique. "Marseille Falls Apart: Why Is France's Second City Crumbling?" *Guardian*, March 21, 2019. https://www.theguardian.com

/cities/2019/mar/21/marseille-falls
-apart-why-is-frances-second-city-
crumbling.

Claude Joseph, Rouget de Lisle. "La
Marseillaise." Strasbourg, 1792.

Cohen, Jean-Louis, and André Lortie.
"Des fortifs au périf." In *Paris, les
seuils de la ville*. Paris: Picard éditeur,
2000.

Collectif du 5 Novembre – Noailles en
colère. "Faites respecter vos droits."
Collectif du 5 Novembre, 2018.
https://collectif5novembre.org/.
Accessed August 7, 2019.

Co-operative Housing International.
Switzerland archives. https://www
.housinginternational.coop/co-ops
/switzerland/. Accessed August
13, 2019.

Crane, Sheila. *Mediterranean Crossroads:
Marseille and Modern Architecture*.
Minneapolis: University of Minnesota
Press, 2011.

Cupers, Kenny. "The Social Project,"
Places Journal, April 2014.
Accessed 14 Jul 2020. https://doi.
org/10.22269/140402

Dearden, Lizzie. "Gunmen in Marseille
'Shoot at Police' Hours before
French Prime Minister Due to Visit."
Independent, February 9, 2015.
https://www.independent.co.uk
/news/world/europe/gunmen-in
-marseille-shoot-at-police-hours
-before-french-prime-minister-due
-to-visit-10033468.html. Accessed
July 1, 2020.

Deboulet, Agnès, and Simone Abram.
"Are Social Mix and Participation
Compatible? Conflicts and Claims
in Urban Renewal in France and
England." In *Social Housing and
Urban Renewal*, edited by Paul
Watt and Peer Smets, 141–77.
Bingley: Emerald, 2017. https://
doi.org/10.1108/978-1-78714-124
-720171003.

De Corbier, Florent. "Marseille: Le sort
des habitants des Crottes supplante la
rénovation." *La Marseillaise*, March
26, 2018. http://m.lamarseillaise.fr
/marseille/societe/68759-le-sort-des
-habitants-supplante-la-renovation.

d'Hombres, Marie, and Blandine Scherer,
*Au 143 rue Félix Pyat: Parc Bellevue,
histoire d'une copropriété à Marseille,
1957–2011* (Aix-en-Provence: REF.
2C éd, 2012).

Dikeç, Mustafa. "Voices into Noises:
Revolts as Unarticulated Justice
Movements." In *Badlands of the
Republic: Space, Politics and Urban
Policy*. Malden, MA: Blackwell,
2007.

Direche, Karima, and Fabienne Le
Houérou. *Les comoriens de Marseille:
D'une mémoire à l'autre*. Paris:
Autrement, 2002.

Dumont, Marie-Jeanne. *Le logement
social à Paris, 1850–1930: Les
habitations à bon marché*. Liège:
Mardaga, 1991.

Durousseau, Thierry. *Ensembles et
résidences à Marseille, 1955–1975*.
Marseille: Bik et Book, 2009.

Durousseau, Thierry. "Marseille XX:
1535–La Castellane." Ministère de la
Culture, 2006. https://www.culture
.gouv.fr/Regions/Drac-Provence
-Alpes-Cote-d-Azur/Politique-et
-actions-culturelles/Architecture
-contemporaine-remarquable-en-Paca
/Les-etudes/Marseille-ensembles-et
-residences-de-la-periode-1955-1975
/Ensembles-residences/Selection-des
-80-ensembles-et-residences/Notices
-monographiques/1535-La-Castellane.
Accessed January 9, 2020.

Durousseau, Thierry. "Marseille 6E–
Le Méditerranée." Ministère de la
Culture, 2006. http://www.culture
.gouv.fr/Regions/Drac-Provence
-Alpes-Cote-d-Azur/Politique-et
-actions-culturelles/Architecture

256

-contemporaine-remarquable
/Le-label/Les-edifices-labellises
/Label-Architecture-contemporaine
-remarquable-Bouches-du-Rhone
/Marseille/Marseille-6e-Le
-Mediterranee. Accessed August 9,
2019.

Durousseau, Thierry. "Marseille 15E–La
Viste." Ministère de la Culture, 2006.
http://www.culture.gouv.fr
/Regions/Drac-Provence
-Alpes-Cote-d-Azur/Politique-et
-actions-culturelles/Architecture
-contemporaine-remarquable
/Le-label/Les-edifices-labellises
/Label-Architecture-contemporaine
-remarquable-Bouches-du-Rhone
/Marseille/Marseille-15e-La-Viste.
Accessed August 9, 2019.

Durousseau, Thierry. "Marseille,
ensembles et résidences de la période
1955/1975." Ministère de la Culture,
2019. http://www.culture.gouv.fr
/Regions/Drac-Provence-Alpes-Cote
-d-Azur/Politique-et-actions
-culturelles/Architecture
-contemporaine-remarquable
/Les-etudes/Marseille-ensembles-et
-residences-de-la-periode-1955-1975.
Accessed August 7, 2019.

Durousseau, Thierry. "Notices
monographiques des 80 ensembles
et résidences étudiés: Les Lierres."
Ministère de la Culture, 2007.
http://www.culture.gouv.fr/Regions
/Drac-Provence-Alpes-Cote-d-Azur
/Politique-et-actions-culturelles
/Architecture-contemporaine
-remarquable/Les-etudes
/Marseille-ensembles-et-residences
-de-la-periode-1955-1975/Ensembles
-residences/Selection-des-80
-ensembles-et-residences/Notices
-monographiques/1213-Les-Lierres.
Accessed August 7, 2019.

Euroméditerranée. "Aménagement
et développement economique à
Marseille." Euroméditerranée.
https://www.Euroméditerranee.fr/.
Accessed August 15, 2019.

Euroméditerranée. "Fabriquer la ville
de demain." Les Fabriques. https://
lesfabriques.fr/. Accessed August 15,
2019.

Firebrace, William. *Marseille Mix.*
London: AA Publications, 2010.

France24. "Chibanis: L'éternel exil des
travailleurs maghrébins." http://
webdoc.france24.com/chibanis
-france-travailleurs-immigration
-maghreb. Accessed August 20, 2019.

Gallent, Nick, and Daniela Ciaffi, eds.
*Community Action and Planning:
Contexts*, Drivers and Outcomes.
Bristol: Policy Press, 2016.

Gilles, Benoît. "Les premiers tronçons
du mur de la Plaine arrivent sur la
place." *Marsactu*, October 30, 2018.
https://marsactu.fr/les-premiers
-troncons-du-mur-de-la-plaine-arrivent
-sur-la-place/?fbclid=IwAR3zzYAnaE9
-KaJOR5I84-xM3Dca_3CsWu9
HpEjpaTHiB-z6ojcjBnp-yeE.%20.

Gilles, Benoît. "N°63 rue d'Aubagne,
symbole de l'inefficacité municipale
contre l'habitat indigne." *Marsactu*,
November 6, 2018. https://marsactu
.fr/n63-rue-daubagne-symbole-de
-linefficacite-municipale-contre
-lhabitat-indigne/?fbclid=IwAR0Mqu
wvaRSPbxcegwMue6U-.

Guinand, Sandra. *Régénérer la ville:
Patrimoine et politiques d'image à
Porto et Marseille.* Rennes: Presses
Universitaires de Rennes, 2015.

Gündogdu, Ayten. "Disagreeing with
Rancière: Speech, Violence, and the
Ambiguous Subjects of Politics."
University of Chicago Press Journals
49, no. 2 (April 2017). https://
www.journals.uchicago.edu/doi
/abs/10.1086/691190.

Haegel, Florence, Henri Rey, and
Yves Sintomer. *La xénophobie en*

banlieue: Effets et expressions. Paris: L'Harmattan, 2000.

Haraway, Donna. "The Promises of Monsters: A Regenerative Politics for Inappropriate/d Others." In The Haraway Reader, edited by Donna Haraway. New York: Routledge, 2004.

Hoad, Phil. "Corrupt, Dangerous and Brutal to Its Poor—but Is Marseille the Future of France?" Guardian, June 8, 2017. https://www.theguardian .com/cities/2017/jun/08/corrupt -dangerous-brutal-poor-marseille -future-france.

Hopquin, Benoît. "La cité Bellevue renaît après dix ans d'abandon." Le Monde, January 23, 2008. https://www.lemonde.fr/municipales -cantonales/article/2008/01/23 /la-cite-bellevue-renait-apres-dix-ans -d-abandon_1002682_987706.html.

Institut national de la statistique et des études économiques. Recensement général de la population. Asnières-sur -Seine: 2013

Institut national de la statistique et des études économiques. Populations communales 2006 en ZUS: Recensement de la population. edited by Insee. Asnières-sur-Seine, 2006.

Izzo, Jean Claude. Total Khéops. Serie Noire. Paris: Editions Gallimard, 1995.

Jolé, Michèle, and William Kornblum. "The Flea Market of Marseille." Metropolitiques, May 17, 2016. https://www.metropolitiques.eu/The -Flea-Market-of-Marseille.html.

L'Etat de Marseille, La Ville de Marseille, Le Collectif du 5 Novembre, Le Conseil citoyen 1/6, Centre ville pour tous L'Association Marseille en Colère, Emmaüs Pointe Rouge, L'Assemblée des délogés, La Fondation Abbé Pierre, Les Compagnons bâtisseurs Provence, L'AMPIL, Destination Famille, and La Ligue des Droits de l'Homme Marseille. Charte de relogement des personnes évacuées. Collectif du 5 Novembre, 2019. https://charte .collectif5novembre.org/. Accessed August 15, 2019.

Laggiard, Fabrice. "Projet de renouvellement urbain." Marseille Renovation Urbaine, January 2018. http://www.marseille-renovation -urbaine.fr/uploads/media /LettreProjetKALLISTE_1_jan18.pdf.

Le centre commercial des Puces de Marseille. "Marché aux puces de Marseille." http://www .centrecommerciallespuces.com/. Accessed August 13, 2019.

Lefebvre, Henri. Espace et politique. Paris: Anthropos, Éditions economica, 1972.

Le Figaro.fr with AFP. "Marseille veut'un nouveau projet urbanistique' rue d'Aubagne." Le Figaro, March 1, 2019. https://www.lefigaro.fr /flash-actu/2019/03/01/97001 -20190301FILWWW00323-marseille -veut-un-nouveau-projet-urbanistique -rue-d-aubagne.php.

Le Garrec, Sylvaine. "Les copropriétés en difficulté dans les grands ensembles: Le cas de Clichy-Montfermeil." Espaces et sociétés 156–57, no. 1 (January 2014): 53–68.

Lees, Johanna. "Les copropriétés dégradées de l'après-guerre à Marseille: Un nouvel habitat social de fait." Espaces et sociétés 156–57, no. 1 (January 2014): 69–84.

Leroux, Luc. "À Marseille, 7 kalachnikovs retrouvées dans la cité de la Castellane après les tirs." Le Monde, February 10, 2015. https://www.lemonde.fr/societe /article/2015/02/09/rafales-d -armes-automatiques-a-marseille -lors-de-la-visite-de-manuel- valls_4572697_3224.html.

Les Associations syndicales. "Qu'est-ce qu'une association syndicale de propriétaires?" L'AD Isère Drac Romanche, July 20, 2008. http://www.isere-drac-romanche.fr/?Qu-est-ce-qu-une-association.

Londres, Albert. *Marseille, porte du sud.* Paris: Arléa, 1999.

Longuenesse, Élisabeth, and Caecilia Pieri. *Des banlieues à la ville.* Beyrouth: Presses de l'Ifpo, 2013.

Marseille autonomous info. "La bataille de la Plaine." *Marseille autonomous info*, October 30, 2018. https://mars-infos.org/la-bataille-de-la-plaine-3470.

Marseille Rénovation Urbaine. "Parc Kallisté." http://www.marseille-renovation-urbaine.fr/kalliste/parc-kalliste-234. Accessed August 8, 2019.

Marseille Rénovation Urbaine. "Ré-urbaniser les copropriétés: Le site de Kallisté." Forum des Projets Urbains, 2018. http://www.projetsurbains.eu. Accessed August 9, 2019.

Maussen, Marcel. "Guest Workers and Islam in France." Chap. 6 in "Constructing Mosques: The Governance of Islam in France and the Netherlands." PhD diss., UVA University Amsterdam, 2009. https://hdl.handle.net/11245/1.311584.

Mazzella, Sylvie. "Le quartier Belsunce à Marseille: Les immigrés dans les traces de la ville bourgeoise." *Les Annales de la Recherche Urbaine* 72, no. 1 (1996): 119−25. doi:10.3406/aru.1996.1987.

McCoy, Alfred W. *Marseille sur héroïne.* Paris: L'Esprit Frappeur, 1999.

Métropole Aix-Marseille-Provence. "Enquête publique." Métropole Aix-Marseille-Provence, accessed August 7, 2019, https://www.marseille-provence.fr/index.php/enquete-publique.

Mézard, Jacques, and Julien Denormandie. "The Three Pillars of the Government's Housing Strategy." Government of France, September 20, 2017. https://www.gouvernement.fr/en/the-government-s-housing-strategy?fbclid=IwAR3ODL-KYmud5GW3-T2ezqVVWQ6PGiyf__aZrtXCgh33SNoyR_x0B6rAcNc.

Moreau, Denis. *Banlieue de Nanterre, le droit a la ville et la périphérie.* Exhibition. Nanterre: Galerie Villa des Tourelles, 2006.

Musée virtuel du logement social. "La cité jardin Saint-Just, à Marseille." Les HLM en Expos. http://musee-hlm.fr/ark:/naan/a011507798835fOC2fb. Accessed August 6, 2019.

Nasiali, Minayo A. "Native to the Republic: Negotiating Citizenship and Social Welfare in Marseille 'Immigrant' Neighborhoods since 1945." PhD diss., University of Michigan, 2010. http://hdl.handle.net/2027.42/77815.

Nicol, Christian. "En matière d'habitat indigne, l'Etat et la Ville ne font pas leur boulot." Interview by Benoît Gilles. *Marsactu*, November 7, 2018. https://marsactu.fr/en-matiere-dhabitat-indigne-letat-et-la-ville-ne-font-pas-leur-boulot/.

Nourisson, Jean-Christophe. *Parc Bellevue XXe siècle: Une oeuvre pour le quartier Saint-Mauront à Marseille.* Paris: Sens & Tonka, 1995.

Panerai, Philippe, Jean Castex, and Jean-Charles Depaule. *Formes urbaines: De l'îlot à la barre.* Collection Aspects de l'urbanisme. Paris: Dunod, 1978.

Patrono, Francesca, Mirko Russo, Claudia Sansú, and Fernand Pouillon. *Fernand Pouillon: Costruzione, Città, Paesaggio.* Napoli: CLEAN edizioni, 2018.

Peraldi, Michel, Claire Duport, and Michel Samson. *Sociologie de Marseille*. Paris: La Découverte, 2015.

Provence 7. "Saint-Just Quartier-Village à visiter." https://www.provence7.com /portails/villes-et-villages/marseille -a-visiter-de-a-a-z/saint-just-quartier -village-a-visiter/. Accessed August 7, 2019.

Pujol, Philippe. *La fabrique du monstre: 10 ans d'immersion dans les quartiers nord de Marseille, la zone la plus pauvre d'Europe*. Paris: Les Arénes, 2015.

Rancière, Jacques. *Dis-agreement: Politics and Philosophy*. Translated by Julie Rose. Minneapolis: University of Minnesota Press, 1999.

Rancière, Jacques. "A Few Remarks on the Method of Jacques Rancière." *Parallax* 15, no. 3 (June 2009): 114–23 doi:10.1080/13534640902982983.

Rancière, Jacques. *The Method of Equality: Interviews with Laurent Jeanpierre and Dork Zabunyan*. Translated by Julie Rose. Cambridge: Polity Press, 2016.

Rice-Oxley, Mark. "Why Are We Building New Walls to Divide Us?" *Guardian*, November 19, 2013. https:// www.theguardian.com/world/ng -interactive/2013/nov/walls#melilla.

Riordan, Christine M. "Diversity Is Useless without Inclusivity." *Harvard Business Review*, June 5, 2014. https://hbr.org/2014/06/diversity-is- useless-without-inclusivity.

Robespierre, Maximilien, and Saint-Just Louis. *Constitution de l'an I*. 1793.

Rodriguez, Alberto, Carl J. Dahlman, and Jamil Salmi. *Knowledge and Innovation for Competitiveness in Brazil*. Washington, DC: World Bank, 2008.

Roncayolo, Marcel. *Lectures de villes: Formes et temps*. Marseille: Editions Parenthèses, 2002.

Rotival, Maurice. "Les grands ensembles." *L'Architecture d'Aujourd'hui* 1, no. 6 (June 1935): 57–72 .

Rough Guide to Provence & the Côte d'Azur, The. London: Penguin Books, 2007.

Rudolph, Nicole. *At Home in Postwar France: Modern Mass Housing and the Right to Comfort*. New York: Berghahn Books, 2015.

Sbriglio, Jacques, and Marie-Helene Biget. *Marseille, 1945–1993*. Marseille: Parenthèses, 1993.

Schwartz, Olivier. "Peut-on parler des classes populaires?" *La vie des idées*, September 13, 2011. https:// laviedesidees.fr/Peut-on-parler-des -classes.html.

Serafini, Tonino. "Logement: À Marseille, Gaudin balaie l'insalubrité sous le tapis." *Libération*, November 8, 2018. https://www.liberation.fr /france/2018/11/08/logement-a -marseille-gaudin-balaie-l-insalubrite -sous-le-tapis_1690931.

Sewell, William H. *Structure and Mobility*. Cambridge: Cambridge University Press, 2009.

Shackney, Elizabeth Joy. "Social Mix or Maquillage? Institutions, Immigration, and Integration in Marseille." MA thesis, Wesleyan University, 2017.

Tellier, Julien. "L'inclusion des quartiers pauvres à travers l'accès aux transports et à l'eau potable." PhD diss., Université de Provence-Aix- Marseille I. Français, 2006. https:// tel.archives-ouvertes.fr/tel-00947479 /file/THESE_Le_Tellier.pdf/.

Témime, Emile, and Pierre Echinard. *Migrance: Histoire des migrations a Marseille*. Volume 4. Aix-en-Provence: Edisud, 1991.

Vidal, Dominique. "Trente ans d'histoire et de révoltes: Banlieue." *Le Monde Diplomatique*, November 2006.

PHOTO CREDITS

Ville de Marseille. "Drame rue d'Aubagne: La Ville de Marseille mobilisée face à l'urgence." March 29, 2019. http://social.marseille .fr/actualites/drame-rue-d-aubagne -la-ville-de-marseille-mobilisee-face-l -urgence.

Vincent, Sébastien. "L'intervention sur les copropriétés dégradées dans les programmes de renouvellement urbain." MA thesis, Institut d'Urbanisme et d'Aménagement Régional d'Aix-en-Provence, 2017. https://dumas.ccsd.cnrs.fr /dumas-01616386/document.

Wiseman, Nicole. "The Construction of Marseille and the Racialized Immigrant." Academia, 2015. https:// www.academia.edu/11575136/The _Construction_of_Marseille_and _the_Racialized_Immigrant.

Zappi, Sylvia. "À Marseille, l'entre-soi d'une cité sans immigrés." *Le Monde*, April 27, 2016. https:// www.org.lemonde.fr/societe /article/2016/02/03/a-marseille -l-entre-soi-d-une-cite-sans -immigres_4858481_3224.html.

p. 38: Monique Hervo and Marie-Ange Charras, Bidonvilles: L'enlisement (Paris: Maspero, 1971).

p. 40: Euroméditerranée, "Plan du périmètre principaux projets et réalisations 2013," accessed March 28, 2018, http://www.Euroméditerranee.fr /fileadmin/templates/plan-du-perimetre .pdf.

p. 42: ZUS (zone urbaine sensible) and QPV (quartier prioritaire de la politique de la ville). © Ancrages.

p. 56: Marine Garand, Julie Freychet, Anansa Gauberti, and Florence Martin, "Les grands ensembles dans le territoire métropolitain," in Ville et territoires (Marseille: Ecole Nationale Supérieure d'Architecture de Marseille, 2014)

p. 206: Euroméditerranée, "Missions," accessed August 14, 2019, https://www .Euroméditerranee.fr/missions.

CONTRIBUTORS

EIRINI AFENTOULI holds a diploma in architecture from the University of Patras, Greece. She contributed to the Venice Architecture Biennale in 2016 and has collaborated with architectural offices in Athens, including Potiropoulos + Partners.

DOYOUNG AHN was born and raised in Seoul, South Korea. After discharge from the Army Corps, he majored in landscape architecture from the University of Idaho (USA) and Seoul National University (South Korea), and worked as a landscape architect and researcher in various offices in South Korea.

JASSIM F. ALNASHMI attained a BArch from Iowa State University and spent a semester at the AA, London. He has worked at firms in the USA and Kuwait, including Perkins + Will. AlNashmi also exhibits his artwork internationally with two collectives, What's Your Location? and Desert Cast.

MARC ANGÉLIL is a professor emeritus in the Department of Architecture at ETH Zurich. His research focuses on the social and spatial development of metropolitan regions across the world. He has authored and coauthored several books, including *Housing Cairo: The Informal Response* (2016), on the informal urbanization of Egypt's capital; *Cidade de Deus! City of God!* (2013), on informal mass housing in Rio de Janeiro; *Indizien* (2006) on the political economy of urban territories; and with Cary Siress, *Mirroring Effects* (2019).

PREETHI ASHOK KUMAR graduated with an architecture degree from Thiagarajar College of Engineering, India. She collaborated with Columbia GSAPP on the "Studio-X" research laboratory exploring the future of cities.

SIMRAN BANSAL graduated with an architecture degree from Bharath University, India. She cofounded Aurazia Design Studio and works on government projects.

BERTA BILBAO VÉLEZ graduated from the Escola Superior d'Arquitectura de Barcelona in 2012. Based in Switzerland since 2013, she works as an architect on public buildings and co-operative housing projects. She was also part of the exhibition design department of MACBA (Museum of Modern Art of Barcelona).

CHIARA CIRRONE graduated with an architecture degree from IUAV in Venice and TU Delft, with the thesis "Living and Working in Addis Ababa: A Proposal for an Alternative Pattern of Inhabitation." She has practiced architecture and urban design in Rotterdam and Tirana.

LUCÍA DEL PIÑAL ÁLVAREZ graduated with an architecture degree in 2016 from the Escuela Superior de Arquitectura de Madrid, specializing in urban planning. She also studied at University of Lund, Sweden, and worked in practices in Madrid and Frankfurt.

THIERRY DUROUSSEAU is a freelance architect investigating urban and architectural heritage. He is a founding member of Mars 26 and the professional association Ordre des Architectes. From 1981 to 1985 he taught at the School of Architecture in Marseille. From 1981 to 2010 he was consultant for the Marseille City Heritage Lab. He is a correspondent for the Heritage Committee of the Académie d'Aix-Marseille.

GE GAO received a master of landscape architecture from the University of Sheffield in 2017. Prior to her studies in England, she earned her bachelor of landscape design at China Academy of Art and worked at AECOM in Shanghai, China, as an urban designer.

GEORGIA GKOTSOPOULOU graduated from the Architecture School of the University of Patras, Greece, and studied abroad at École Nationale Supérieure d'Architecture de Saint-Étienne. She contributed to the Venice Architecture Biennale in 2010 and collaborated with the architecture studio Drifting City, Athens.

ANDREA GONZÁLEZ PALOS holds a master's degree in urbanism from KTH Stockholm and a bachelor's degree in architecture from Universidad Iberoamericana, Mexico. She has practiced as an architect and urban designer specializing in mapping, spatial analysis, participatory urbanism, and place-making.

DHRUV GUSAIN graduated from the Department of Architecture at the Sarvajanik College of Engineering and Technology, Surat, India (2015). He has worked on institutional and urban design projects with Vastu-Shilpa consultants in Ahmedabad and on private houses with his own practice.

AKASH JOSHI graduated from Kamla Raheja Vidyanidhi Institute for Architecture in Mumbai (2015). He has worked with RMA Architects (Boston+Mumbai) and various architecture and urban design offices in India. He practices independently on interior, architecture, and urban-scale projects.

CAROL KAN holds a master of architecture from SCI-Arc (2017) in Los Angeles and a bachelor of architectural studies with a minor in economics from

Carleton University (2014) in Ottawa. She has collaborated with studios in North America, Europe, and Asia.

STEFANIA KONTINOU-CHIMOU graduated with an architecture degree from University of Patras, Greece. During her studies, she collaborated with 314architecturestudio in Athens and B612associates in Brussels, focusing on private and social housing as well as commercial and cultural projects.

FAI LEELASIRIWONG graduated with an architecture degree from Chulalongkorn University in Bangkok. She is based in Thailand, working with A49 on public buildings and with Chat Architects, where she also participated in the research project "Bangkok Bastards" investigating the city's urban conditions.

JIN LI holds a bachelor's degree in architecture from the Shandong Jianzhu University in China and studied as an exchange student at the AA School of Architecture in London. She also worked at Kengo Kuma's office and with Studio FUKSAS in China.

PABLO LEVINE MARDONES graduated with an architecture degree from Pontificia Universidad Catolica de Chile. Since his graduation he has been practicing independently and won and realized several competitions in urban and architectural practice.

JULIE DE MUER is a writer and cultural producer based in Marseille since 2003. Until 2009 she was director of Radio Grenouille and the sound creation workshop Euphonia. In the context of Marseille-Provence 2013 European Capital Year of Culture, she accompanied and cofounded several territorial projects.

She is currently involved in the field of social innovation with 27e Région.

VIRGINIA MALAMI graduated in 2015 from the Technical University of Crete's School of Architecture as a scholar of the National Scholarship Foundation of the Technical University of Crete and Gazi-Triantaffylopoulos Foundation, after an exchange semester at IUAV Venice.

CHARLOTTE MALTERRE-BARTHES is an architect and associate professor of urban design at the Harvard Graduate School of Design. She holds a doctoral degree from ETH Zurich on food and territories and directed the MAS Urban Design from 2014 to 2019. She is coauthor with Marc Angélil of *Cairo Desert Cities* (2018) and *Housing Cairo: The Informal Response* (2016), and principal of the urban design office OMNIBUS, dedicated to new forms of practice. In 2019, she cocurated the 12th International Architecture Biennale of São Paulo.

BEATRICE MELONI graduated in architecture from Politecnico di Torino. She studied as an exchange student at Istanbul Technical University where she completed her master's thesis, and has collaborated with different design offices in Italy.

NICOLAS MEMAIN is an urbanist without a diploma. He is a member of the Cercle des Marcheurs and cartographer of the GR2013®. In 2013 he received the prize of Urban Planning of the Academy of Architecture for the creation of a metropolitan path. As a specialist in urban planning and architecture of the twentieth century, he organized architectural walks in several municipalities of Bouches-du-Rhone and participated in an architectural inventory of heritage services. In 2020, he was elected municipal councillor for the first district of Marseille.

MARIA OROZCO AGUIRRE holds a master of architecture with a specialization in urbanism from the Polytechnic University of Catalonia, Barcelona. She practiced in Guayaquil, Ecuador, where she completed her undergraduate degree in architecture at Espiritu Santo University.

GEORGE PAPADIMAS KAMPELIS holds a diploma in architecture from the National Technical University of Athens. His diploma project, "Crisis Question," was exhibited at the Venice Architecture Biennale in 2016. He collaborated with Dionisis Sotovikis Workshop and completed several architecture projects in Greece and Cyprus.

RIMA PATEL graduated in architecture from CEPT University in Ahmedabad, India, with an exchange semester in VSVU, Slovakia. Along with her independent practice, she has worked on several projects with the architect Kishore Trivedi. She has taught at the Indubhai Parekh School of Architecture Rajkot.

CAITANYA PATEL graduated in architecture from Maharaja Sayajirao University in Baroda, India. Along with his independent practice, he has worked at Sangath with Balkrishna Doshi in Ahmedabad, where he collaborated with Shigeru Ban Architects on a project in Amaravati.

CHRYSOYLA PIERRAKOU holds a five-year diploma in architecture from the University of Thessaly. She has worked at architecture offices in Greece such as MOB architects.

KALLIOPI SAKELLAROPOULOU received a master of architecture from University of Patras in 2017 where she worked as a researcher for the εNaf Research program (2014–19). She has worked in several architecture offices in Greece on private projects and public competitions.

ALEXIS SCHULMAN graduated from the Ecole Spéciale d'Architecture, Paris, in 2009. He won the CIAF prize in the XI Forum of Young Architects (2013) in Kosice, Slovakia. He has practiced as an architect in France, Mexico, and Ecuador.

WENJIE SHEN graduated from the South China University of Technology in 2017. She also interned at the Tsinghua University design institute and ATKINS in Beijing.

CARY SIRESS is senior researcher at ETH Zurich. His work on territorial organization at the Future Cities Laboratory in Singapore focuses on global urbanization processes. He is guest professor in urban design at the Nanjing University Graduate School of Architecture and Urban Planning in China. His previous publications include *Hard Plan – Soft City*, which investigates the "city as designed" versus the "city as used," and with Marc Angélil, *Mirroring Effects* (2019).

SOMETHING FANTASTIC is an undisciplinary architecture office founded by Leonard Streich, Julian Schubert, and Elena Schütz. The firm's agenda is based on the idea that architecture is affected by everything and vice versa—does affect everything—and therefore working as architects implies a broad interest and involvement in the world. Something Fantastic's practice includes designing books, exhibitions, furniture, buildings, and urban development schemes. Next to designing, the partners write, lecture, art direct, and teach. Since 2019 they direct the Studio for Immediate Spaces at Gerrit Rietveld Academie's Sandberg Instituut in Amsterdam, and from 2012 to 2019 they taught the MAS Urban Design at ETH Zurich. In 2016 the studio was responsible for the design of the German Pavilion at the 15th La Biennale di Venezia entitled "Making Heimat: Germany, Arrival Country."

ALEXIOS TSAKALAKIS-KARKAS holds a diploma in architecture from the University of Patras, Greece. He has collaborated with acclaimed Greek architecture offices such as Point Supreme Architects, Papalampropoulos Syriopoulou Architecture Bureau, and Klab Architects.

GRIGORIOS TSANTILAS received a diploma in architecture from the University of Thessaly in 2015. He studied as an exchange student at the Faculdades de Arquitectura e Artes das Universidades Lusíada, Lisbon, in 2012. He has practiced architecture in Berlin.

CHRISTINA TZEVELEKOU received a diploma in architecture from National Technical University of Athens. She has worked as an architect for R.C.TECH and as a freelancer in Athens on urban and housing projects. She contributed to the Venice Architecture Biennale in 2016 with her diploma project.

MARIANA VARGAS MONDRAGÓN studied architecture at Instituto Tecnologico de Estudios Superiores de Monterrey in Queretaro, Mexico. Upon graduation in 2013 she initiated her practice m2Studio, and has also collaborated with Vargas Construction Co. in California since 2009.

ACKNOWLEDGMENTS

ALEXANDRA ZACHARIADI holds a diploma in architecture from the University of Patras, Greece. During her studies, she worked as an intern architect at K2A architecture office in Brussels, Belgium, and at A2 architects in Athens, Greece.

YIHAN ZHANG holds a BArch degree from Changsha University of Science and Technology, China. She has participated in several architectural competitions and workshops related to sustainable architecture and encoding formation. She has worked in different offices in China.

The MAS class of 2016–17 contributed ideas to the present publication: Bo Wang, Yen-Cheng Chen, Dimitra Christoforidi, Valerio Ciaccia, Vasiliki Daskalaki, Alaa Dia, Lama El Masri, Ahmed Eltobgy, Michele Fumagalli, Hsuan-Tung Lin, Zafeiris Magarakis, Sofia Georgia Tzereme, Konstantinos Tzioras, David Benjamin Vogel, Hee-Young Yoon, Miao Yu, Pacharapan Ratananakorn, Siyuan Shi, and Rodi Tsitouridou.

The MAS Urban Design classes of 2017–19 and the teaching team would like to thank the following people, structures, and institutions who facilitated in one way or another the work in Marseille and Zurich:

Marseille: Carole Barthelemy, Laura Bernardini, Matthias Bourrissoux, Centre ville pour tous, Château en santé, Elsa Clérin, Thierry Durousseau, Ymane Fakhir, M. Findt, Foresta, Patrick Lacoste, Fabrice Laggiard, Magali Launay, LPED, Tifawt Loudaoui, Maisons de Marseille, Nicolas Memain, Myriame Morel, Lea Ortolli, Mathieu Poitevin, Fanny Privat, Ecole de la Jougarelle, Coco Velten, Yes We Camp

Ancrages: Guy Battini, Saïda Belaïd, Toufik Belmehdi, Samia Chabani, Anaëlle Chauvet, André Donzel, Hanane Kesraoui, Marina Sanchez

Bureau des guides du GR2013: Marielle Agboton, Alexandre Field, Loic Magnant, Julie Demuer, Marion Bottaro

Le Cabanon Vertical: Olivier Bedu

Hôtel du Nord: Fati, Rachid Rahmouni

Migrantour: Steve Manny

Pamplemousses Enflammés: Noël Cauchi, Julie Fallot

MAS Junior Assistants: Lukas Graf, Sara Sherif

Special thanks to Sascha Delz

Thanks to: Nishat Awan, Sandra Bartoli, Monica Basbous, Wulf Böer, Barbara Costa, Kim Courrèges, Matthew Critchley, Irina Davidovici, Guillermo Dürig, Eiffage-Immobilier, Emily Eliza

Scott, Daniel Fernández Pascual, Felipe
de Ferrari, Kim Förster, Hans Frei,
Alejandra Fries, Romina Grillo, Harry
Gugger, Gide Haider, Mona Harb,
Tanja Herdt, Alice Hertzog, Ilmar
Hurkxkens, Katja Jug, Nikos Katsikis,
Anne Kockelkorn, Christoph Kueffer,
Anne Lacaton, Nikos Magouliotis, Ciro
Miguel, Gyler Mydyti, Sarah Nichols,
Daniela Ortiz dos Santos, Eva Pfannes,
Public Works, Jenny Rodenhouse,
Sascha Roesler, Miro Roman, Gabrielle
Schaad, Christian Schmid, Alon Schwabe,
Dubravka Sekulić, Cary Siress, Anna-
Sophie Springer, Linda Stagni, Fernanda
Tellez Velasco, Alfredo Thiermann, Milica
Topalović, Jason W. Moore

Le Maire
Ancien Ministre
président honoraire du Sénat

Arrêté N° 2019_00202_VDM

SDI 18/276 - ARRÊTÉ DE PÉRI[...]T - 40, RUE D'AUBAGNE - 13001 - 201803 B0079

Nous, Maire de Marseille,

Vu l'article L.2131.1 du code géné[...] [...]tivités territoriales,
Vu les articles L.511.1 à L.511.6, a[...] [...]rticles L.521.1 à L.521.4 du code de la construction
et de l'habitation, (Annexe 1)
Vu les articles R.511.1 à R.511.5 du [...] [...]onstruction et de l'habitation,
Vu l'article R.556.1 du code de jus[...] [...]rative,
Vu l'arrêté de délégation de fonc[...] [...]ie par le Maire n°14/252/SG du 14 avril 2014, à
Monsieur Ruas en matière notamm[...] [...]e des Immeubles menaçant ruine et d'insécurité des
équipements communs des immeu[...] [...]s à usage principal d'habitation,
Vu l'avis réputé favorable de l'arch[...] [...]timents de France,
Vu le rapport de visite du 20 d[...] [...]18 de Monsieur Michel COULANGE, Architecte
D.P.L.G. expert désigné par ordo[...] [...]Madame le Président du Tribunal Administratif de
Marseille sur notre requête,

Considérant l'immeuble sis 40 rue [...] 13001 MARSEILLE, parcelle cadastrée n° 201803
B0079 – Quartier Noailles, appa[...] [...]n nos informations à ce jour, en copropriété aux
personnes listées en Annexe 2, ou [...] [...] droit,

Considérant le syndicat des cop[...] [...]de cet immeuble pris en la personne du Cabinet
QUITTARD Immobilier, domicilié [...] [...]ceau, 13005 MARSEILLE,

Considérant l'évacuation, pour [...] [...]sécurité, des occupants de l'immeuble lors de
l'intervention d'urgence du 23 nove[...]

Considérant l'avertissement notifi[...] [...]mbre 2018 au syndicat des copropriétaires de cet
immeuble pris en la personne du [...] [...]ITTARD Immobilier, domicilié 6 rue du Berceau,
13005-MARSEILLE,

Considérant le rapport d'experti[...] [...]reconnaissant l'état de péril grave et imminent,
constatant les pathologies suivante[...]

     - des coulures im[...] [...]des fuites sur les réseaux sont visibles dans la cave,
     - les poutrelles [...] [...]constituant le plancher haut de la cave sont
partiellement dég[...] [...]rouille
     - le plafond du d[...] [...]itué sous la toiture s'écroule en plusieurs endroits
     - la toiture est trè[...] [...]encombrée (tuiles manquantes, déplacées)
     - l'enduit de la fa[...] [...] des boursouflures

Ville de Marse[...] [...]ort - 13233 MARSEILLE CEDEX 20

Article 13   Le [...]
dans [...]

ENTRESOL

Пушење убија.
вански дим штети
удима у Вашој
околини.

COLOPHON

Migrant Marseille
Architectures of Social Segregation
and Urban Inclusivity

The content of this publication was
realized by students of the Master of
Advanced Studies in Urban Design at
ETH Zurich. The program was initiated
by the Chair of Professor Marc Angélil in
the Department of Architecture.

Editors: Marc Angélil,
Charlotte Malterre-Barthes,
Julian Schubert, Elena Schütz,
Leonard Streich

Concept: Charlotte Malterre-Barthes
and Something Fantastic (Julian Schubert,
Elena Schütz, Leonard Streich)

Design: Something Fantastic Art Dept.
with Fernanda Tellez Velasco

Copyediting: Max Bach, Jaqueline Taylor

Printing: Nomos, Germany

MAS Urban Design teaching team:
Charlotte Malterre-Barthes,
Something Fantastic (Julian Schubert,
Elena Schütz, Leonard Streich),
Sascha Delz

Typeface: Arial, Life Regular,
Life Regular Italic

Paper: Enso 60g Lux Cream

Die Deutsche Bibliothek lists
this publication in the Deutsche
Nationalbibliographie. Detailed
bibliographic data is available on the
internet at www.dnb.de.

This publication was made possible by
the generous support of: ETH Zurich,
Department of Architecture.

www.angelil.arch.ethz.ch

Ruby Press
Schönholzer Str. 13-14
10115 Berlin
Germany

www.ruby-press.com

Printed in Germany
ISBN: 978-3-944074-33-7